Complete Horoscope

Capricorn 2023

Monthly astrological forecasts for 2023

TATIANA BORSCH

Translated from Russian by Sonja Swenson
Translation copyright © Coinflow Limited, Cyprus
AstraArt Books is an imprint of Coinflow limited, Cyprus
Published by Coinflow Limited, Cyprus
For queries please contact: tatianaborsch@yahoo.com

ISBN978-9925-609-01-7(paperback)
ISBN 978-9925-609-02-4(ebook)

Contents

2023 –The Great Transition Continues 5

2023 Overview for Capricorn...............................11

January 13

February 16

March 19

April 22

May 25

June 28

July 31

August 34

September 37

October...40

November 43

December 46

Capricorn Description...49

A Guide to The Moon Cycle and Lunar Days.......................52

A Guide to Zodiac Compatibility 81

Love Description of Zodiac Signs...............................89

2023 –The Great Transition Continues

In previous forecasts, I have described the unique transition period in which the world finds itself.

I will summarize for those who have not read my predictions for 2020, 2021, and 2022.

We have entered a period of changes, and the world has come to a fateful point, where everything that seemed constant and unshakable no longer is. If that is the case, then what awaits us?

From an astrological perspective, 2020, 2021, and 2022 are extensions of one long period, and cannot be divided. This is a time of major changes in every nation, home, and individual.

There is no comparison for this period in modern history. In fact, humanity has not lived through a period quite like this for a very long time.

The astrological explanation for this is that we are living through a grandiose shift in eras. The Age of Pisces, which lasted for 2,160 years, is transitioning into the Age of Aquarius.

2023 fits naturally into this complex sequence. This is an important and critical watershed.

During the first half of 2023, we see a natural continuation of a very complicated period that began in 2022. The confrontation between East and West will continue in Ukraine, as will rivalry between the United States and China, along with financial and economic crises that have beset the entire world.

As of June 2022, when this forecast is being written, I can predict that in the fall of 2022, that is in October and November, the conflict between Russia and the West in Ukraine will reach a new level. Russia's advancements will force the West, including the United States, to take on a more active role in the face of the invasion in Ukraine, as the entire world risks being dragged into a new war.

The stars predict that the war in Ukraine may come to an end in January-February 2023. Ukraine will be divided into two zones of influence, with much of its territory falling under Russia's shadow. Volodymyr Zelenskyy will lose his grip on power and may flee the country, and Ukrainian leadership will be replaced. Peace initiatives that might otherwise be capable of changing this tragic situation will constantly be thwarted. In January 2023, aggressive Mars will no longer be in retrograde, and by February, there will be a light at the end of the tunnel. Initially, it will be just a flicker, but it is certainly better than nothing.

Gradually, the countries involved in this conflict will come to realize that they need to hold constructive negotiations in order to meet all of society's healthy demands and trends. These talks will not be swift, and they will probably only bear fruit in the second half of 2023.

Overall, despite Ukraine's valiant efforts both militarily and politically, along with support from the West, Russia will prevail, militarily, geopolitically, and ideologically.

This will seriously alter the geopolitical landscape on the global stage. In time, Asia and Russia will dominate the world's economy. The events of this year are just one more step in the transition as global influence shifts eastward. Tensions between the United States and Asian countries will only heat up.

In late 2022 and early 2023, many countries' economies will descend into chaos, and a general financial crisis will drag down banks, companies, and the entire planet's population.

In many Western countries, antiwar sentiment will be palpable, and there may be demonstrations, protests, and other expressions of dissatisfaction with governments.

In Russia, the fall of 2022 and first half of 2023 will see widespread changes in the structures of power. Western sanctions will lead to serious economic losses, forcing Russia to find a way to survive in the face of Western and American economic aggression.

The worst economic crisis will take place in the United States. The fall of 2022 and during the first half of 2023 may be the worst period it has faced in recent memory. There may be serious confrontations between political parties, which might throw American society as a whole off balance. During the fall of 2022 and first half of 2023, President Biden will experience serious difficulties. The stars predict he will face worsening health, along with serious destabilization of the entire American financial system. (A president's horoscope is responsible for much of what will happen to his or her country). During the same period, Bident's great foe, former President Trump, is expected to become much more active and powerful.

European countries will not be spared, either. In France, opposition to President Macron's policies will grow and Macron will lose some of his influence.

In Germany, Chancellor Olaf Scholz will become more aggressive during the fall. Despite his outward calm, he may turn out to be an active supporter of Western support for Ukraine. This will lead to a backlash in German society, and by May 2023, Scholz will be in a much weaker position than he is today.

From November 2022 to May 2023, the United Kingdom may see changes in leadership. This will be a period full of obstacles, including serious financial difficulties, demonstrations by those who disagree with the political power structure, and a trend of separatism in the various regions. In June-July, things will calm down significantly, and the British financial and political system will manage to recover.

The second half of May will also be a time of challenges. Jupiter will square Pluto during this time, with support from aggressive Mars. We can expect cataclysms and changes in many countries' governments here. Serious acts of terrorism cannot be ruled out, either.

During the second half of 2023, Jupiter will transition from the bellicose sign of Aries into the more peaceful sign of Taurus, and its favorable aspect with Saturn in June gives reason to hope that things are likely to improve.

That process will not be overnight, however. We see evidence of that in Uranus, which will be in the sign of Taurus, at the same degrees as during the period of World War II. Taurus symbolizes life and all its peaceful manifestations, while Uranus is the symbol of renewal through destruction. That portends a break with old structures, which may unleash war, death, and political and economic clashes.

All of these painful processes will eventually lead to the birth of a new, modern world, but that will not be completed until after 2025.

Looking at the future, I predict that in late 2022, and early 2023, economic, political, and social, as well as personal crises will reach a peak. Remember, we are blessed to live in an era of great change, and historical events certainly do leave their mark on our personal lives.

I also predict that during the second half of 2023, we will reach the halfway point on this long and winding road, and this may be the most complicated part of that trajectory. After this point, people will begin looking for a way to resolve the world's most pressing problems, and the light at the end of the tunnel may start to glimmer a bit brighter. Of course, this is inevitable, but step by step, people will start to tackle the many challenges we face. This is a gradual, sometimes painful process. But there is hope that Fate will have less unpleasant surprises in store for us and life will start running a bit more smoothly. It will never go back to exactly the way it was, but as this period draws to a close, we will see that in one way or another, all of these changes are for the best.

Money

We may face a global banking system crisis, which is likely to happen in November-December 2022. I believe it would be wiser to hold your money in something tangible, like real estate, land, or gold, than in the banking system or simply on paper. Purchasing power may experience a serious decline.

Health

Health-wise, anyone with thyroid problems or cardiovascular disease or any illnesses involving the blood vessels of the brain should be particularly cautious. We see this as Uranus transits into Taurus.

Pluto is still in Capricorn, which exacerbates musculoskeletal and bone disorders. Teeth are also in Pluto's crosshairs, so it is best to treat them quickly!

Cancer cases may rise, so do not hesitate to visit the doctor quickly, as cancer is only treatable in the early stages.

In 2023, Saturn is transiting into Pisces – this may lead to problems for those with various types of diabetes or problems involving the legs.

During the spring and fall of 2023, more outbreaks of unknown diseases and viruses are possible.

Nature

In 2023, various natural anomalies that the world has been struggling with may continue. Jupiter in Aries might cause fires, which will be a destabilizing factor during the winter and spring of 2023.

However, in early May, when Jupiter transitions into Taurus, we can expect to see significant improvements in agriculture. Harvests will be more abundant, which, in many countries, will mean a way out of the food crisis. Many countries will also be able to invest more in agriculture production and processing, which will only revive small towns and villages.

Fashion

Jupiter will be in Aries during the first half of 2023, and this promises all shades of red, which will be on models everywhere during this period. Many people will instinctively be drawn to red, as Aries's energy simply hangs in the air. Military-inspired dress may also be on the runways.

During the second half of 2023, Jupiter will transition into Taurus, which is primarily green in color. This is a great color, as it symbolizes growth and rebirth. Taurus's second color is pink, which symbolizes romanticism, softness, love for sensual pleasures and enjoyment. The fashion world may respond in kind with light, floaty fabrics and perhaps a new focus on femininity.

Have a wonderful year! Don't be afraid of crises, as they bring with them new opportunities!

Always,

Tatiana Borsch

2023 Overview for Capricorn

The time has come to take care of yourself and those you love. That is what the stars are urging you to do in 2023. Your home is your castle, and right now, that's what you need to keep in mind.

Work. This year is relatively smooth sailing for you. No major career changes are on the horizon, but you are sure to have a lot of work on your hands. During the first half of the year, you will see a continuation of the events from 2022.

Business owners and managers will still be expanding their business, and that will involve a whole host of administrative tasks. That may involve repairs and other events related to acquiring facilities, land, or other real estate. In some cases, that may be taking place in another city or abroad.

A few problems that began last fall will still be felt in January. This will be one of the hardest periods of 2023. However, closer to March, the most difficult matters will be resolved, one way or another, and they won't bother you anymore.

Your connections with colleagues from other cities or abroad will be moving along with varying success, however, here is where you will manage to recover much of what was lost.

Employees will manage to dedicate more time to their family, and perhaps things are so stable and calm at work, and many of your headaches from last year are no longer so pressing.

During the second half of the year, you will experience a dynamic, creative period. You will have a wonderful opportunity to demonstrate your talents to a wider audience, along with official bodies.

Those who work in creative fields – actors, musicians, artists, and anyone who works with words – will see particular success.

During the second half of the year, the most difficult months for anything work-related will be November and December. During this time, you will experience disagreements with friends, like-minded people, or those highly placed in society. However, by the holidays, all of this will be behind you.

Money. Financially, you will be ready for the unexpected, whether good or bad, though there more be more of the bad. You will be spending constantly, and the end of July will be particularly egregious, as will August and November. The astrologist predicts that much of this will be in your personal life, family, or due to your children's needs.

Love and family. 2023 will bring many events to your personal life. During the first half, many Capricorns will be busy setting up their home, maybe for themselves, or possibly for their children.

Your children bring you joy, and they are finally on the positive streak you have been waiting for. They will need your efforts, however, whether financial or other forms of support. In many families, you will welcome new children or grandchildren.

Couples will feel like they are on a rollercoaster this month, and that will be most palpable during the period from August to November. If you have any unresolved issues in your relationship, they may spill over this time, and force you to make a decision – it's now or never. Remember that a happy ending isn't only for fairytales, and sometimes, we get one in real life, too. The most important thing is to remember that it's all up to you.

Health. All year long, you are feeling energetic and even illnesses from 2022 will quickly fade away.

January

New York Time			London Time		
Calendar Day	Lunar Day	Lunar Day Start Time	Calendar Day	Lunar Day	Lunar Day Start Time
01/01/2023	11	12:58 PM	01/01/2023	10	12:31 PM
02/01/2023	12	1:32 PM	02/01/2023	11	12:56 PM
03/01/2023	13	2:10 PM	03/01/2023	12	1:27 PM
04/01/2023	14	2:53 PM	04/01/2023	13	2:05 PM
05/01/2023	15	3:42 PM	05/01/2023	14	2:51 PM
06/01/2023	16	4:36 PM	06/01/2023	15	3:45 PM
07/01/2023	17	5:32 PM	07/01/2023	16	4:45 PM
08/01/2023	18	6:31 PM	08/01/2023	17	5:50 PM
09/01/2023	19	7:30 PM	09/01/2023	18	6:56 PM
10/01/2023	20	8:29 PM	10/01/2023	19	8:04 PM
11/01/2023	21	9:28 PM	11/01/2023	20	9:11 PM
12/01/2023	22	10:28 PM	12/01/2023	21	10:19 PM
13/01/2023	23	11:29 PM	13/01/2023	22	11:28 PM
15/01/2023	24	12:32 AM	15/01/2023	23	12:40 AM
16/01/2023	25	1:38 AM	16/01/2023	24	1:54 AM
17/01/2023	26	2:47 AM	17/01/2023	25	3:11 AM
18/01/2023	27	3:56 AM	18/01/2023	26	4:28 AM
19/01/2023	28	5:05 AM	19/01/2023	27	5:42 AM
20/01/2023	29	6:08 AM	20/01/2023	28	6:46 AM
21/01/2023	30	7:02 AM	21/01/2023	29	7:38 AM
21/01/2023	1	3:55 PM	21/01/2023	1	8:55 PM
22/01/2023	2	7:49 AM	22/01/2023	2	8:17 AM
23/01/2023	3	8:28 AM	23/01/2023	3	8:48 AM
24/01/2023	4	9:01 AM	24/01/2023	4	9:13 AM
25/01/2023	5	9:32 AM	25/01/2023	5	9:34 AM
26/01/2023	6	10:01 AM	26/01/2023	6	9:54 AM
27/01/2023	7	10:30 AM	27/01/2023	7	10:14 AM
28/01/2023	8	11:00 AM	28/01/2023	8	10:35 AM
29/01/2023	9	11:33 AM	29/01/2023	9	11:00 AM
30/01/2023	10	12:10 PM	30/01/2023	10	11:29 AM
31/01/2023	11	12:52 PM	31/01/2023	11	12:04 PM

You can find the description of each lunar day in the chapter "A Guide to The Moon Cycle and Lunar Days"

It seems you are once again planning a real estate transaction, and as usual, things are very serious! Ride the wave!

Work. For many Capricorns, the holidays will be over, and you will be back to work by January 4 or 5.

All month long, entrepreneurs and managers of every level will have to grapple with problems on their team. The disagreements may have begun earlier, in the fall or winter of 2022. There may have been a mutiny, or perhaps someone behaving unscrupulously or simply being incompetent. The situation is now coming to an end. You will have to reach an agreement with someone, but it is not worth counting on certain individuals.

Employees may once again be seeing changes at work, which may have begun in the summer of 2022. For now, things have stabilized, though some will decide to leave, and others will find great benefits to staying where they are.

The best time to resolve your greatest and most complicated work-related problems is the last 10 days of the month. The first 20 days, you would do better to study the situation and discuss it in detail. Many things may look unclear and uncertain during this time.

Money. Overall, your finances are stable. You will have a steady income, thanks to Venus, which is moving into the financial sector of your sky all month.

Expect the greatest sums to come in on January 3, 4, 13, 14, 22, 23, 30, and 31. Your expenses are low, and mostly related to your personal life – vacation and your loved ones' needs.

Love and family. You are seeing changes in your personal life once again. They may look differently – it all depends on your past relationship and your future plans. Partners who have a strong relationship will solve problems related to their housing or other real estate together.

Those who are ready to split up will also be dealing with housing-related issues, either giving them up or dividing them.

Your relationship with relatives is also shifting. Longstanding disputes and other problems are coming to a close. One or both sides will eventually realize that a bad peace is better than a good war, and act accordingly.

It is hard to say what is in store for those who are dating. Their relationship might not be defined yet, or perhaps it will come to some kind of close. There may be some minor disagreements, and getting over them will require wisdom, patience, and understanding. But the most important factor is love, and the rest, they say, will follow.

Health. In January, you are not feeling very energetic. And there is a strong chance of old or unexpected diseases rearing their ugly heads. If you had health problems in the fall and winter of 2022, you may still be dealing with lingering troubles. This will not last, and the stars predict changes for the better.

February

New York Time			London Time		
Calendar Day	Lunar Day	Lunar Day Start Time	Calendar Day	Lunar Day	Lunar Day Start Time
01/02/2023	12	1:38 PM	01/02/2023	12	12:48 PM
02/02/2023	13	2:30 PM	02/02/2023	13	1:39 PM
03/02/2023	14	3:26 PM	03/02/2023	14	2:37 PM
04/02/2023	15	4:24 PM	04/02/2023	15	3:41 PM
05/02/2023	16	5:23 PM	05/02/2023	16	4:47 PM
06/02/2023	17	6:22 PM	06/02/2023	17	5:54 PM
07/02/2023	18	7:22 PM	07/02/2023	18	7:02 PM
08/02/2023	19	8:22 PM	08/02/2023	19	8:10 PM
09/02/2023	20	9:22 PM	09/02/2023	20	9:19 PM
10/02/2023	21	10:24 PM	10/02/2023	21	10:28 PM
11/02/2023	22	11:27 PM	11/02/2023	22	11:40 PM
13/02/2023	23	12:33 AM	13/02/2023	23	12:54 AM
14/02/2023	24	1:40 AM	14/02/2023	24	2:09 AM
15/02/2023	25	2:46 AM	15/02/2023	25	3:22 AM
16/02/2023	26	3:50 AM	16/02/2023	26	4:28 AM
17/02/2023	27	4:47 AM	17/02/2023	27	5:24 AM
18/02/2023	28	5:36 AM	18/02/2023	28	6:09 AM
19/02/2023	29	6:19 AM	19/02/2023	29	6:44 AM
20/02/2023	1	2:09 AM	20/02/2023	1	7:09 AM
20/02/2023	2	6:55 AM	20/02/2023	2	7:11 AM
21/02/2023	3	7:28 AM	21/02/2023	3	7:35 AM
22/02/2023	4	7:58 AM	22/02/2023	4	7:56 AM
23/02/2023	5	8:28 AM	23/02/2023	5	8:16 AM
24/02/2023	6	8:59 AM	24/02/2023	6	8:38 AM
25/02/2023	7	9:32 AM	25/02/2023	7	9:02 AM
26/02/2023	8	10:08 AM	26/02/2023	8	9:30 AM
27/02/2023	9	10:49 AM	27/02/2023	9	10:03 AM
28/02/2023	10	11:34 AM	28/02/2023	10	10:44 AM

You can find the description of each lunar day in the chapter "A Guide to The Moon Cycle and Lunar Days"

Once again, money is on your mind. Here, there is nothing you can do about it, – for you, material success is a must.

Work. This month, many Capricorns are consumed with the busywork of expanding their business, especially upper-level managers and business owners. However, not everything will go as planned. During the first 10 days of February, you can expect petty work-related disagreements and conflicts with colleagues and subordinates.

Those planning to do business with partners from other cities or abroad will face obstacles during this time.

These issues are unlikely to have lasting consequences, and during the last 20 days of the month, they are sure to be favorably resolved.

Employees might argue with gossipy colleagues during the first 10 days of the month. The stars remind you that silence is golden and avoid adding to the intrigue – it's better this way.

During the last 20 days of the month, things are much more promising. Many of your problems will disappear, and your work will continue to move forward in your favor.

Money. February is a good time for your wallet. Money will be coming in regularly, and you will have enough of it to cover your growing expenses.

Expect the largest sums to come in on February 1, 9-11, 18, 19, 27, and 28.

The largest expenses will take placed during the first few days of the month, and the stars predict that they will mostly be related to your children's needs.

Love and family. Your personal life will be sharply focused on your living space, this month. Many Capricorns will be busy with home improvements, whether for themselves or their children. You may also acquire more real estate.

Unmarried couples will go through a rough patch until February 10. Arguments are likely, and you may be the cause. Try to keep a lid on your emotions and avoid throwing any temper tantrums. At least remember that your actions have consequences.

During the first 10 days of the month, you may experience problems when it comes to your relatives. The cause may be something that came up in the recent past, so there is nothing new here.

For various reasons, trips planned for the first 10 days of February might not take place or might turn out differently than you had expected.

Health. For most of February, you are feeling sluggish, so try to take care of yourself and lead a healthy lifestyle.

March

New York Time			London Time		
Calendar Day	Lunar Day	Lunar Day Start Time	Calendar Day	Lunar Day	Lunar Day Start Time
01/03/2023	11	12:24 PM	01/03/2023	11	11:33 AM
02/03/2023	12	1:19 PM	02/03/2023	12	12:29 PM
03/03/2023	13	2:16 PM	03/03/2023	13	1:31 PM
04/03/2023	14	3:15 PM	04/03/2023	14	2:36 PM
05/03/2023	15	4:15 PM	05/03/2023	15	3:44 PM
06/03/2023	16	5:14 PM	06/03/2023	16	4:52 PM
07/03/2023	17	6:15 PM	07/03/2023	17	6:00 PM
08/03/2023	18	7:15 PM	08/03/2023	18	7:09 PM
09/03/2023	19	8:17 PM	09/03/2023	19	8:19 PM
10/03/2023	20	9:20 PM	10/03/2023	20	9:31 PM
11/03/2023	21	10:25 PM	11/03/2023	21	10:44 PM
13/03/2023	22	12:31 AM	12/03/2023	22	11:58 PM
14/03/2023	23	1:37 AM	14/03/2023	23	1:11 AM
15/03/2023	24	2:40 AM	15/03/2023	24	2:18 AM
16/03/2023	25	3:37 AM	16/03/2023	25	3:16 AM
17/03/2023	26	4:28 AM	17/03/2023	26	4:03 AM
18/03/2023	27	5:12 AM	18/03/2023	27	4:41 AM
19/03/2023	28	5:50 AM	19/03/2023	28	5:10 AM
20/03/2023	29	6:23 AM	20/03/2023	29	5:35 AM
21/03/2023	30	6:54 AM	21/03/2023	30	5:57 AM
21/03/2023	1	1:26 PM	21/03/2023	1	5:26 PM
22/03/2023	2	7:24 AM	22/03/2023	2	6:17 AM
23/03/2023	3	7:55 AM	23/03/2023	3	6:38 AM
24/03/2023	4	8:27 AM	24/03/2023	4	7:01 AM
25/03/2023	5	9:03 AM	25/03/2023	5	7:28 AM
26/03/2023	6	9:43 AM	26/03/2023	6	9:00 AM
27/03/2023	7	10:27 AM	27/03/2023	7	9:38 AM
28/03/2023	8	11:16 AM	28/03/2023	8	10:25 AM
29/03/2023	9	12:10 PM	29/03/2023	9	11:19 AM
30/03/2023	10	1:07 PM	30/03/2023	10	12:19 PM
31/03/2023	11	2:05 PM	31/03/2023	11	1:24 PM

You can find the description of each lunar day in the chapter "A Guide to The Moon Cycle and Lunar Days"

Seeking inner and outer harmony may take you around the world. But somewhere, you will try to put down roots.

Work. The lion's share of March will be dedicated to organizational tasks. Business owners and managers might work on expanding their business, and this will involve looking at acquiring new facilities. If this already happened recently, you will spend the next few months getting the property ready for operations. In some cases that will take place in another city or abroad and may involve some travel.

The good news is that many of the administrative tasks you have planned for March are expected to go smoothly, without any hiccups.

Nothing is perfect, however, and managers might run into problems with their subordinates, as well as some disagreements with colleagues from afar over business issues.

Employees might experience conflict with a colleague and are advised to listen more than they talk. Do not engage unless you have iron-clad arguments and facts on your side.

All of these unpleasant encounters are expected during the second 10 days of the month. The first and last 10 days will be in your favor.

Money. March will be very kind to your wallet. In addition to your usual income, you can count on the proceeds of various real estate transactions or a profitable sale. In addition, you may receive credit, support from your parents, or an elder family member.

Love and family. In many cases, most of the action this month will involve your home and family. Many Capricorns will be busy with the purchase or renovation of a new home, apartment, summer house, possibly in a place far away from where you live now.

The family ambiance is warm and comfortable, which has not always been the case in the last several years. In some cases, spouses might have finally reached a solution that suits them both, while in others, divorce will have gone smoothly for everyone. Without a heavy burden to carry around, you are able to finally take a leap forward and meet your new destiny.

Your relationship with relatives is full of ups and downs, especially during the second 10 days of the month, when petty disagreements and blow-outs alike are to be expected. This may become chronic, so be careful and look for the weak parts of your relationships and take steps to fix them.

Any trips planned for March will be a success, as long as they are planned during the first and last 10 days of the month. During the second 10 days, things are less auspicious, but you have no choice, be sure to take care of your documents and observe the laws of any foreign countries.

Health. This month, you are healthy and energetic, but the stars remind you to be extra cautious when driving or behind the wheel!

April

New York Time		
Calendar Day	Lunar Day	Lunar Day Start Time
01/04/2023	12	3:04 PM
02/04/2023	13	4:04 PM
03/04/2023	14	5:04 PM
04/04/2023	15	6:05 PM
05/04/2023	16	7:07 PM
06/04/2023	17	8:11 PM
07/04/2023	18	9:16 PM
08/04/2023	19	10:23 PM
09/04/2023	20	11:30 PM
11/04/2023	21	12:34 AM
12/04/2023	22	1:33 AM
13/04/2023	23	2:25 AM
14/04/2023	24	3:10 AM
15/04/2023	25	3:48 AM
16/04/2023	26	4:22 AM
17/04/2023	27	4:53 AM
18/04/2023	28	5:22 AM
19/04/2023	29	5:52 AM
20/04/2023	1	12:15 AM
20/04/2023	2	6:23 AM
21/04/2023	3	6:57 AM
22/04/2023	4	7:35 AM
23/04/2023	5	8:18 AM
24/04/2023	6	9:06 AM
25/04/2023	7	9:59 AM
26/04/2023	8	10:55 AM
27/04/2023	9	11:53 AM
28/04/2023	10	12:52 PM
29/04/2023	11	1:52 PM
30/04/2023	12	2:51 PM

London Time		
Calendar Day	Lunar Day	Lunar Day Start Time
01/04/2023	12	2:30 PM
02/04/2023	13	3:38 PM
03/04/2023	14	4:46 PM
04/04/2023	15	5:56 PM
05/04/2023	16	7:06 PM
06/04/2023	17	8:18 PM
07/04/2023	18	9:32 PM
08/04/2023	19	10:47 PM
10/04/2023	20	12:02 AM
11/04/2023	21	1:11 AM
12/04/2023	22	2:12 AM
13/04/2023	23	3:02 AM
14/04/2023	24	3:41 AM
15/04/2023	25	4:12 AM
16/04/2023	26	4:38 AM
17/04/2023	27	5:00 AM
18/04/2023	28	5:20 AM
19/04/2023	29	5:40 AM
20/04/2023	1	5:15 AM
20/04/2023	2	6:02 AM
21/04/2023	3	6:27 AM
22/04/2023	4	6:56 AM
23/04/2023	5	7:32 AM
24/04/2023	6	8:15 AM
25/04/2023	7	9:07 AM
26/04/2023	8	10:06 AM
27/04/2023	9	11:09 AM
28/04/2023	10	12:15 PM
29/04/2023	11	1:23 PM
30/04/2023	12	2:30 PM

You can find the description of each lunar day in the chapter "A Guide to The Moon Cycle and Lunar Days"

You are moving toward the goals you set for yourself, and the path ahead is open. You have dealt with many obstacles. Some are behind you, but those that are left will be easily overcome.

Work. Once again, the main theme of this month is developing your relationship with colleagues in other cities or abroad. In April, you may hold successful negotiations on cooperation, or discuss major financial and administrative issues. Some Capricorns will be busy setting up facilities to expand their business, and you will be able to assess your capabilities and get a clear-eyed view of the location you have selected.

In some cases, you might count on support from relatives, and this is especially true if you have a family business.

Employees might consider various options for employment in a company that has many ties to other cities or abroad. The stars welcome any opportunity to study somewhere faraway.

Money. Your financial situation is gradually normalizing. The major expenses that were so frequent during the last few months are no longer an issue. Saturn, the planet of limitations, discipline, and modesty is now in the sector of the sky responsible for finances, and that may drive a sense of responsibility in anything related to money. Keep a close eye on your budget and avoid any unnecessary spending. But given your cautious nature, you probably don't need to be told.

Love and family. If the major events of this year are taking place in your personal life, this is where you will see a shift. Many Capricorns will be busy with various real estate transactions, possibly related to a move to another city or abroad, or alternatively, simply to a new home. Most likely, all of these related events in April are in the planning phase, and it will take some time for your plans to come to life.

Your relationship with your children is more predictable, and the worst is probably behind you. Ahead, expect smooth sailing and for the difficulties of the last few months to be over.

Divorcing couples might manage to discuss material issues in relative peace, and if you can, try to deal with the thorniest issues this month, while you have an opportunity for both sides to reach a compromise.

Your relatives' influence in family problems can only be positive right now.

Couples will have a calm April, and things will be predictable. You might discuss the future of your relationship or possibly living together.

Health. In April, you are feeling energetic. You are active, vibrant, and able to bring your ideas to life in business and at home.

May

New York Time			London Time		
Calendar Day	Lunar Day	Lunar Day Start Time	Calendar Day	Lunar Day	Lunar Day Start Time
01/05/2023	13	3:52 PM	01/05/2023	13	3:39 PM
02/05/2023	14	4:53 PM	02/05/2023	14	4:48 PM
03/05/2023	15	5:56 PM	03/05/2023	15	6:00 PM
04/05/2023	16	7:02 PM	04/05/2023	16	7:14 PM
05/05/2023	17	8:09 PM	05/05/2023	17	8:30 PM
06/05/2023	18	9:18 PM	06/05/2023	18	9:47 PM
07/05/2023	19	10:25 PM	07/05/2023	19	11:00 PM
08/05/2023	20	11:27 PM	09/05/2023	20	12:06 AM
10/05/2023	21	12:22 AM	10/05/2023	21	1:01 AM
11/05/2023	22	1:10 AM	11/05/2023	22	1:43 AM
12/05/2023	23	1:50 AM	12/05/2023	23	2:16 AM
13/05/2023	24	2:24 AM	13/05/2023	24	2:43 AM
14/05/2023	25	2:55 AM	14/05/2023	25	3:05 AM
15/05/2023	26	3:24 AM	15/05/2023	26	3:25 AM
16/05/2023	27	3:53 AM	16/05/2023	27	3:45 AM
17/05/2023	28	4:23 AM	17/05/2023	28	4:05 AM
18/05/2023	29	4:55 AM	18/05/2023	29	4:28 AM
19/05/2023	30	5:31 AM	19/05/2023	30	4:55 AM
19/05/2023	1	11:55 AM	19/05/2023	1	4:55 PM
20/05/2023	2	6:11 AM	20/05/2023	2	5:27 AM
21/05/2023	3	6:57 AM	21/05/2023	3	6:08 AM
22/05/2023	4	7:48 AM	22/05/2023	4	6:56 AM
23/05/2023	5	8:44 AM	23/05/2023	5	7:53 AM
24/05/2023	6	9:42 AM	24/05/2023	6	8:55 AM
25/05/2023	7	10:41 AM	25/05/2023	7	10:01 AM
26/05/2023	8	11:40 AM	26/05/2023	8	11:07 AM
27/05/2023	9	12:39 PM	27/05/2023	9	12:14 PM
28/05/2023	10	1:38 PM	28/05/2023	10	1:22 PM
29/05/2023	11	2:38 PM	29/05/2023	11	2:30 PM
30/05/2023	12	3:39 PM	30/05/2023	12	3:40 PM
31/05/2023	13	4:43 PM	31/05/2023	13	4:52 PM

You can find the description of each lunar day in the chapter "A Guide to The Moon Cycle and Lunar Days"

May is a challenging and unusual time for you. You may be an incorrigible workaholic, but the stars urge you to busy yourself with your love life or family. This month will be interesting but emotionally taxing.

Work. Though most of the month will have you busy with your personal affairs, you will not stop working altogether. The best time for work-related matters is the last 10 days of May, when all of your working processes will be close to complete, whether you are an employee or business owner.

During the first 20 days of the month, you may run into some problems and obstacles. You may get a way to relax, and if you do stick around at work, the people you need will not be nearby.

The good news in all of this is that you will renew your ties with your business partners in other cities or abroad. Most likely, these are connections you made some time ago, and which for some reason petered out.

Those busy with expanding their business might complete the initial tasks related to this.

Money. Financially, May might be difficult for you. You can expect major expenses, higher than your income, mostly related to your personal life and home and children's needs.

Your children may be responsible for the lion's share of this spending.

Love and family. Your personal life is at the heart of it all this month! Perhaps you will manage to keep a lid on your innate conservatism and try your hand at something romantic. It will not be difficult for you to steal the hearts of those around you with your brilliant wit and talents on full display. This is a great chance to find just the right person, if you haven't found him or her just yet.

Those with families will be immersed in their children's affairs, and this will likely involve a serious investment in their education and training.

The first 20 days of May are a good time for renewing your relationships. For various reasons listed above, the last 10 days are a good time to meet new people. For the rest of the year, your life will become much freer, more interesting, and romantic.

You might finally get a handle on your household issues, and finally able to focus on much more pleasant tasks.

Health. In May, you are healthy, energetic, looking great, and impressing everyone Fate sends your way.

June

New York Time			London Time		
Calendar Day	Lunar Day	Lunar Day Start Time	Calendar Day	Lunar Day	Lunar Day Start Time
01/06/2023	14	5:50 PM	01/06/2023	14	6:07 PM
02/06/2023	15	6:59 PM	02/06/2023	15	7:24 PM
03/06/2023	16	8:08 PM	03/06/2023	16	8:41 PM
04/06/2023	17	9:14 PM	04/06/2023	17	9:52 PM
05/06/2023	18	10:14 PM	05/06/2023	18	10:53 PM
06/06/2023	19	11:06 PM	06/06/2023	19	11:41 PM
07/06/2023	20	11:50 PM	08/06/2023	20	12:19 AM
09/06/2023	21	12:27 AM	09/06/2023	21	12:48 AM
10/06/2023	22	12:59 AM	10/06/2023	22	1:11 AM
11/06/2023	23	1:29 AM	11/06/2023	23	1:32 AM
12/06/2023	24	1:57 AM	12/06/2023	24	1:52 AM
13/06/2023	25	2:26 AM	13/06/2023	25	2:11 AM
14/06/2023	26	2:56 AM	14/06/2023	26	2:33 AM
15/06/2023	27	3:30 AM	15/06/2023	27	2:57 AM
16/06/2023	28	4:08 AM	16/06/2023	28	3:27 AM
17/06/2023	29	4:51 AM	17/06/2023	29	4:04 AM
18/06/2023	1	12:39 AM	18/06/2023	30	4:49 AM
18/06/2023	2	5:40 AM	18/06/2023	1	5:39 AM
19/06/2023	3	6:34 AM	19/06/2023	2	5:42 AM
20/06/2023	4	7:31 AM	20/06/2023	3	6:43 AM
21/06/2023	5	8:30 AM	21/06/2023	4	7:47 AM
22/06/2023	6	9:29 AM	22/06/2023	5	8:54 AM
23/06/2023	7	10:28 AM	23/06/2023	6	10:01 AM
24/06/2023	8	11:27 AM	24/06/2023	7	11:07 AM
25/06/2023	9	12:25 PM	25/06/2023	8	12:14 PM
26/06/2023	10	1:25 PM	26/06/2023	9	1:22 PM
27/06/2023	11	2:27 PM	27/06/2023	10	2:32 PM
28/06/2023	12	3:31 PM	28/06/2023	11	3:44 PM
29/06/2023	13	4:37 PM	29/06/2023	12	4:59 PM
30/06/2023	14	5:46 PM	30/06/2023	13	6:15 PM

You can find the description of each lunar day in the chapter "A Guide to The Moon Cycle and Lunar Days"

He who would eat the fruit must climb the tree. If that is your motto this month, you will go far.

Work. In June, many Capricorns will have to draw a clear line between their professional and personal lives, and your presence will be sine qua non, here.

Business owners and managers will have to deal with matters related to production, and it is absolutely essential that your team's work be coordinated and coherent, here.

Many will have to smooth over a relationship with colleagues in other cities or abroad, which will require skill and effort on your part. You are sure to succeed in part, and the rest will require hard work. You may need to turn to a mediator or attorney in order to get a full handle on things.

You will need to prepare meticulously for any business travel planned for June, and study all possibilities, including those that are less than favorable. However, despite a few bobbles, things will move forward, and nothing will seriously throw a wrench in your plans.

Money. Your financial outlook is contradictory this month. On one hand, you will have your usual income, but you will also be bleeding money. The astrologist predicts that most of this will be related to your personal life, family, and your children's and loved ones' needs.

Expect to spend the greatest amounts in mid to late June.

Those who work with others' finances – accountants, bankers, and brokers – should be especially careful in June. Avoid any risky financial operations, as they will bring major losses, rather than profit.

Love and family. In June, your personal life is no less important than work. Parents will be dealing with their children's troubles and spend a lot of money on their development and education. Your children will bring you joy, and they are continuing to experience a positive streak.

Spouses whose marriage is on the rocks will clash yet again, this time over finances. Material matters are coming to a head for those who recently decided to divorce.

Your relationship with relatives may be challenging, as well. In some cases, that may mean things have cooled off or someone has been alienated. You are likely to reach a compromise, so there is reason to assess the situation and make the most beneficial choice you can.

Health. This month, you are feeling tired, but if you lead a healthy lifestyle and don't overdo things, you will avoid any complications.

July

New York Time		
Calendar Day	Lunar Day	Lunar Day Start Time
01/07/2023	15	6:54 PM
02/07/2023	16	7:58 PM
03/07/2023	17	8:55 PM
04/07/2023	18	9:44 PM
05/07/2023	19	10:25 PM
06/07/2023	20	11:00 PM
07/07/2023	21	11:31 PM
09/07/2023	22	12:01 AM
10/07/2023	23	12:29 AM
11/07/2023	24	12:59 AM
12/07/2023	25	1:32 AM
13/07/2023	26	2:08 AM
14/07/2023	27	2:49 AM
15/07/2023	28	3:36 AM
16/07/2023	29	4:28 AM
17/07/2023	30	5:24 AM
17/07/2023	1	2:33 PM
18/07/2023	2	6:22 AM
19/07/2023	3	7:21 AM
20/07/2023	4	8:20 AM
21/07/2023	5	9:19 AM
22/07/2023	6	10:17 AM
23/07/2023	7	11:15 AM
24/07/2023	8	12:15 PM
25/07/2023	9	1:16 PM
26/07/2023	10	2:20 PM
27/07/2023	11	3:26 PM
28/07/2023	12	4:33 PM
29/07/2023	13	5:39 PM
30/07/2023	14	6:39 PM
31/07/2023	15	7:32 PM

London Time		
Calendar Day	Lunar Day	Lunar Day Start Time
01/07/2023	14	7:30 PM
02/07/2023	15	8:37 PM
03/07/2023	16	9:33 PM
04/07/2023	17	10:16 PM
05/07/2023	18	10:49 PM
06/07/2023	19	11:15 PM
07/07/2023	20	11:38 PM
08/07/2023	21	11:58 PM
10/07/2023	22	12:18 AM
11/07/2023	23	12:39 AM
12/07/2023	24	1:02 AM
13/07/2023	25	1:30 AM
14/07/2023	26	2:04 AM
15/07/2023	27	2:46 AM
16/07/2023	28	3:36 AM
17/07/2023	29	4:34 AM
17/07/2023	1	7:33 PM
18/07/2023	2	5:37 AM
19/07/2023	3	6:43 AM
20/07/2023	4	7:50 AM
21/07/2023	5	8:56 AM
22/07/2023	6	10:03 AM
23/07/2023	7	11:09 AM
24/07/2023	8	12:17 PM
25/07/2023	9	1:27 PM
26/07/2023	10	2:39 PM
27/07/2023	11	3:53 PM
28/07/2023	12	5:07 PM
29/07/2023	13	6:16 PM
30/07/2023	14	7:17 PM
31/07/2023	15	8:07 PM

You can find the description of each lunar day in the chapter "A Guide to The Moon Cycle and Lunar Days"

Expect a positive month, divided into two halves. There's both good news and bad news. But the stars predict that you will manage it all!

Work. During the first 20 days of July, you can be sure to ride a positive streak. During this time, work will move at a comfortable pace, without any hold ups or problems. You will renew your ties with colleagues from other cities or abroad, and you may take a successful trip. You are at the heart of it all – you are surrounded by old colleagues and new friends. Negotiations are going as they should, and you are showing everyone you are positive and knowledgeable. This is a great time for exchanging any information, studies, and communications.

After July 20, things will grow more complicated. During this time, the connections you have built will unexpectedly fail. Initially, this involves colleagues from other cities or abroad. Here, you can expect various misunderstandings, so keep your finger on the pulse of what's happening and consider various options to get back on the straight and narrow.

During the same time, you can expect various financial challenges, which will include unexpected expenses, debts, and spending on hospitality.

Money. Financially speaking, the first 20 days of the month will be neutral. You will have your normal income, and your spending will be reasonable and modest. During the last 10 days of July, however, expect to grapple with business expenses, debts, and spending related to your personal life.

Love and family. Some Capricorns will be more focused on their personal life this month. You may head somewhere with a warm, sunny beach, and spend time with relatives or friends who live in other cities or abroad.

During the first 20 days of July, your relationship with relatives is fairly calm, and if you had any recent misunderstandings, they will be resolved. But don't let your guard down – during the last 10 days of the month, you might find yourself arguing once again. Don't be surprised if all of your family members get dragged into it, as well.

During the last 10 days of July, you might also face problems related to your children. In the best-case scenario, that just means expenses related to their education, studies, and development whether they are still small or already grown. In the worst cases, though, expect to tangle over money with your adult children.

During the last 10 days of July, couples can expect trouble, as well. Fate's path is at times confusing. Something that seemed clear is not so anymore. The problem might be you and your inner problems and have nothing to do with your partner. If that sounds like you, assess the situation and do not make any final decisions. Venus, the planet of love, is in retrograde, and this is not the time to exert full control over the situation or try to force any understanding. If you have any doubts, just sit tight!

Health. This month, you are feeling sluggish, though you will not fall ill. Close to the end of the month, many Capricorns might feel tired from meetings, negotiations, or being surrounded by people. In late July or August, it will be time to take a break.

During the last 10 days of the month, be extra careful when driving or traveling. There is a high probability of accidents on the road during this time.

August

New York Time		
Calendar Day	Lunar Day	Lunar Day Start Time
01/08/2023	16	8:17 PM
02/08/2023	17	8:56 PM
03/08/2023	18	9:30 PM
04/08/2023	19	10:01 PM
05/08/2023	20	10:31 PM
06/08/2023	21	11:01 PM
07/08/2023	22	11:33 PM
09/08/2023	23	12:09 AM
10/08/2023	24	12:49 AM
11/08/2023	25	1:34 AM
12/08/2023	26	2:24 AM
13/08/2023	27	3:18 AM
14/08/2023	28	4:16 AM
15/08/2023	29	5:14 AM
16/08/2023	1	5:38 AM
16/08/2023	2	6:13 AM
17/08/2023	3	7:12 AM
18/08/2023	4	8:10 AM
19/08/2023	5	9:09 AM
20/08/2023	6	10:08 AM
21/08/2023	7	11:08 AM
22/08/2023	8	12:10 PM
23/08/2023	9	1:13 PM
24/08/2023	10	2:18 PM
25/08/2023	11	3:22 PM
26/08/2023	12	4:23 PM
27/08/2023	13	5:18 PM
28/08/2023	14	6:06 PM
29/08/2023	15	6:48 PM
30/08/2023	16	7:24 PM
31/08/2023	17	7:57 PM

London Time		
Calendar Day	Lunar Day	Lunar Day Start Time
01/08/2023	16	8:45 PM
02/08/2023	17	9:15 PM
03/08/2023	18	9:40 PM
04/08/2023	19	10:02 PM
05/08/2023	20	10:22 PM
06/08/2023	21	10:44 PM
07/08/2023	22	11:07 PM
08/08/2023	23	11:33 PM
10/08/2023	24	12:05 AM
11/08/2023	25	12:44 AM
12/08/2023	26	1:32 AM
13/08/2023	27	2:27 AM
14/08/2023	28	3:29 AM
15/08/2023	29	4:34 AM
16/08/2023	30	5:41 AM
16/08/2023	1	10:38 AM
17/08/2023	2	6:47 AM
18/08/2023	3	7:54 AM
19/08/2023	4	9:00 AM
20/08/2023	5	10:07 AM
21/08/2023	6	11:16 AM
22/08/2023	7	12:25 PM
23/08/2023	8	1:37 PM
24/08/2023	9	2:49 PM
25/08/2023	10	3:59 PM
26/08/2023	11	5:02 PM
27/08/2023	12	5:56 PM
28/08/2023	13	6:38 PM
29/08/2023	14	7:12 PM
30/08/2023	15	7:39 PM
31/08/2023	16	8:03 PM

You can find the description of each lunar day in the chapter "A Guide to The Moon Cycle and Lunar Days"

August might test your strength, but that's no reason to cry over spilled milk. Concrete actions are better for you than fanciful expectations that your problems will solve themselves.

Work. As often happens, you can expect to face a dilemma this summer – to relax in style or put your nose to the grindstone? The stars suggest that you will manage to do both but remain focused on all fronts and don't lose sight of the details.

Those with ties to colleagues in other cities or abroad may yet again face challenges in August. Perhaps there are financial demands or expenses that have been unaccounted for.

Negotiations in this area may go on all month long, and perhaps even into September. In some cases, you may even find yourself in legal proceedings. In time, things will resolve themselves, and that is most likely to happen in September or October. For now, do what you need to do and don't rush – the key to fixing anything right now is paying special attention to detail.

Money. Expect August to be a ruinous time for you. You will be spending constantly, perhaps due to work, or possibly vacations and y our personal life. Either way, control your spending and avoid any financial risks right now. That goes for both money and anything of material value.

Love and family. For many Capricorns, August is a time for resolving thorny issues in your personal life, too. Parents will support their children's education, development, and growth, which requires a lot of resources.

You can expect problems involving relatives to continue, and the cause depends on the past.

Couples will come to a major crossroads – will they remain together or separate forever?

All month long, Venus is in retrograde, and the last 10 days of August,

Mercury will join it. That means that decision-making will be difficult, and maybe it's best to put things off until later. In time, the planets will calm down and you will see things in new light.

Alternatively, you may decide to separate for some time, and perhaps that is not such a bad idea, after all.

Health. This month, you are feeling tired, so take care of yourself and find some time to relax. You will have the opportunity to do just that. However, if you wish to go somewhere, select a place you have been several times before, and be mindful of other countries' laws.

All month long, take care when driving!

September

New York Time			London Time		
Calendar Day	Lunar Day	Lunar Day Start Time	Calendar Day	Lunar Day	Lunar Day Start Time
01/09/2023	18	8:28 PM	01/09/2023	17	8:24 PM
02/09/2023	19	8:59 PM	02/09/2023	18	8:46 PM
03/09/2023	20	9:32 PM	03/09/2023	19	9:09 PM
04/09/2023	21	10:07 PM	04/09/2023	20	9:34 PM
05/09/2023	22	10:46 PM	05/09/2023	21	10:05 PM
06/09/2023	23	11:30 PM	06/09/2023	22	10:43 PM
08/09/2023	24	12:19 AM	07/09/2023	23	11:28 PM
09/09/2023	25	1:13 AM	09/09/2023	24	12:21 AM
10/09/2023	26	2:09 AM	10/09/2023	25	1:21 AM
11/09/2023	27	3:08 AM	11/09/2023	26	2:25 AM
12/09/2023	28	4:07 AM	12/09/2023	27	3:31 AM
13/09/2023	29	5:05 AM	13/09/2023	28	4:38 AM
14/09/2023	30	6:04 AM	14/09/2023	29	5:45 AM
14/09/2023	1	9:40 PM	15/09/2023	1	2:40 AM
15/09/2023	2	7:03 AM	15/09/2023	2	6:52 AM
16/09/2023	3	8:02 AM	16/09/2023	3	7:59 AM
17/09/2023	4	9:02 AM	17/09/2023	4	9:07 AM
18/09/2023	5	10:03 AM	18/09/2023	5	10:16 AM
19/09/2023	6	11:06 AM	19/09/2023	6	11:27 AM
20/09/2023	7	12:10 PM	20/09/2023	7	12:39 PM
21/09/2023	8	1:13 PM	21/09/2023	8	1:48 PM
22/09/2023	9	2:13 PM	22/09/2023	9	2:52 PM
23/09/2023	10	3:09 PM	23/09/2023	10	3:48 PM
24/09/2023	11	3:58 PM	24/09/2023	11	4:33 PM
25/09/2023	12	4:41 PM	25/09/2023	12	5:09 PM
26/09/2023	13	5:18 PM	26/09/2023	13	5:38 PM
27/09/2023	14	5:52 PM	27/09/2023	14	6:03 PM
28/09/2023	15	6:24 PM	28/09/2023	15	6:25 PM
29/09/2023	16	6:55 PM	29/09/2023	16	6:46 PM
30/09/2023	17	7:27 PM	30/09/2023	17	7:08 PM

You can find the description of each lunar day in the chapter "A Guide to The Moon Cycle and Lunar Days"

September might seem quieter and more productive than the previous months. Good times are ahead!

Work. Things will be picking up again at work this month. Though you may have a lot of clouds on the horizon before September 15, during the second half of the month, the sky will clear.

You might be holding negotiations with colleagues in other cities or abroad during the first half of the month, and perhaps you are preparing for a trip. Mercury, the planet that rules connection and contacts will be in retrograde until September 15, so be prepared for the fact that things may not turn out as you hoped the first time around. You will have to reexamine some things, and perhaps even redo them.

However, during the second half of the month, everything will be complete, and you will be pleased with the results.

Your negotiations with colleagues from afar are on the right track, and closer to the end of September, you will get what you wanted.

During this time, Capricorns might suddenly become very popular within their own circles. You can expect visits and interesting, useful events – seminars, symposiums, and creative gatherings. You will show your best side and make new connections. Those who work in the creative fields will see the most success here – actors, artists, journalists, musicians, and of course, politicians. As your popularity grows, so will your income.

Money. The last 10 days of September is the best time for your finances. You can expect the largest sum to come in on September 25-27.

Your expenses are still high, and most of them are still related to your family's needs and those of your children and loved ones.

Love and family. Things will improve in your personal, romantic, and family life during the second half of September.

Couples will find a way to one another's hearts, and the stars urge you to go on a trip together. This will strengthen your relationship and allow you to see things from another perspective.

Spouses will improve their relationship with children, though that will still require a lot of money.

If you have any plans related to travel, be careful with your documents, and carefully study any maps before setting out. This month, try to choose places you have been a few times before. This is valid all month long, especially during the first half, and for any business travel.

Health. In September, you are feeling great about yourself, and any illness from last month will swiftly be but a bad memory.

October

New York Time			London Time		
Calendar Day	Lunar Day	Lunar Day Start Time	Calendar Day	Lunar Day	Lunar Day Start Time
01/10/2023	18	8:02 PM	01/10/2023	18	7:33 PM
02/10/2023	19	8:40 PM	02/10/2023	19	8:02 PM
03/10/2023	20	9:23 PM	03/10/2023	20	8:38 PM
04/10/2023	21	10:11 PM	04/10/2023	21	9:21 PM
05/10/2023	22	11:04 PM	05/10/2023	22	10:12 PM
07/10/2023	23	12:01 AM	06/10/2023	23	11:11 PM
08/10/2023	24	12:59 AM	08/10/2023	24	12:14 AM
09/10/2023	25	1:58 AM	09/10/2023	25	1:20 AM
10/10/2023	26	2:57 AM	10/10/2023	26	2:27 AM
11/10/2023	27	3:56 AM	11/10/2023	27	3:34 AM
12/10/2023	28	4:54 AM	12/10/2023	28	4:40 AM
13/10/2023	29	5:54 AM	13/10/2023	29	5:48 AM
14/10/2023	30	6:54 AM	14/10/2023	30	6:56 AM
14/10/2023	1	1:55 PM	14/10/2023	1	6:55 PM
15/10/2023	2	7:55 AM	15/10/2023	2	8:06 AM
16/10/2023	3	8:59 AM	16/10/2023	3	9:17 AM
17/10/2023	4	10:03 AM	17/10/2023	4	10:29 AM
18/10/2023	5	11:07 AM	18/10/2023	5	11:40 AM
19/10/2023	6	12:08 PM	19/10/2023	6	12:46 PM
20/10/2023	7	1:05 PM	20/10/2023	7	1:44 PM
21/10/2023	8	1:55 PM	21/10/2023	8	2:32 PM
22/10/2023	9	2:38 PM	22/10/2023	9	3:09 PM
23/10/2023	10	3:16 PM	23/10/2023	10	3:40 PM
24/10/2023	11	3:50 PM	24/10/2023	11	4:05 PM
25/10/2023	12	4:21 PM	25/10/2023	12	4:27 PM
26/10/2023	13	4:51 PM	26/10/2023	13	4:48 PM
27/10/2023	14	5:22 PM	27/10/2023	14	5:09 PM
28/10/2023	15	5:55 PM	28/10/2023	15	5:32 PM
29/10/2023	16	6:32 PM	29/10/2023	16	4:59 PM
30/10/2023	17	7:13 PM	30/10/2023	17	5:31 PM
31/10/2023	18	8:00 PM	31/10/2023	18	6:11 PM

You can find the description of each lunar day in the chapter "A Guide to The Moon Cycle and Lunar Days"

October will be a month of strong will and determination for you. You are taking Fate into your own strong hands and confirming the rules of the game you think are necessary.

Work. For anything work-related, October is one of the best months of 2023 for you. Finally, you will have a chance to make some of your plans a reality, and you are very enthusiastic about your work. However, the stars believe that your fantasies often exceed your financial possibilities.

Your relationship with colleagues in other cities or abroad is once again becoming important and your progress here is encouraging. Minor disagreements are possible in mid-October, but you will overcome them favorably.

Employees can count on good will from their managers, additional responsibilities, and some pleasant financial perks.

The best time for anything work-related is the first 20 days of October. During the last 10 days, a fog will suddenly gather on your hitherto sunny horizon.

The lunar eclipse on October 28 will bring a series of problems involving friends or someone highly placed in society. This may be over money or your excessive independence. As you charge ahead, you can expect these problems to follow you into November.

Money. Financially, October is a great time for you. You will have regular income and significantly more of it than usual. Expect the largest sums to come in on October 3, 4, 13, 14, 22, 23, and 31.

Most of your expenses will take place during the last 10 days of October, and the astrologist they will be related to your personal life and your children's and loved ones' needs.

Love and family. Everything is going swimmingly in your personal life. Your relationship with your children is becoming easier and improving, and you might find common ground with your adult children or solve any problems involving younger ones.

Couples are in for a pleasant surprise in October. If you recently had an argument, you will reconcile. However, pay attention to everything around you and keep your emotions in check – during the last 10 days of the month, you might argue yet again.

Though things are looking up until October 20, you should try to resolve any unanswered quandaries during that time, in order to begin the difficult last 10 days of the month with a clean slate.

Your relationship with relatives is still not ideal, and you may find yourself constantly grappling with petty disagreements. This will continue for some time, so try to find a way out, and things are likely to resolve in your favor. Of course, that will require the will and patience to do that.

Health. You are energetic, active, and the picture of health in October.

November

New York Time				London Time		
Calendar Day	Lunar Day	Lunar Day Start Time		Calendar Day	Lunar Day	Lunar Day Start Time
01/11/2023	19	8:52 PM		01/11/2023	19	7:00 PM
02/11/2023	20	9:49 PM		02/11/2023	20	7:57 PM
03/11/2023	21	10:47 PM		03/11/2023	21	9:00 PM
04/11/2023	22	11:47 PM		04/11/2023	22	10:06 PM
05/11/2023	23	11:46 PM		05/11/2023	23	11:13 PM
07/11/2023	24	12:45 AM		07/11/2023	24	12:20 AM
08/11/2023	25	1:43 AM		08/11/2023	25	1:26 AM
09/11/2023	26	2:42 AM		09/11/2023	26	2:33 AM
10/11/2023	27	3:42 AM		10/11/2023	27	3:41 AM
11/11/2023	28	4:43 AM		11/11/2023	28	4:50 AM
12/11/2023	29	5:46 AM		12/11/2023	29	6:02 AM
13/11/2023	1	4:27 AM		13/11/2023	30	7:15 AM
13/11/2023	2	6:51 AM		13/11/2023	1	9:27 AM
14/11/2023	3	7:57 AM		14/11/2023	2	8:28 AM
15/11/2023	4	9:01 AM		15/11/2023	3	9:38 AM
16/11/2023	5	10:00 AM		16/11/2023	4	10:40 AM
17/11/2023	6	10:53 AM		17/11/2023	5	11:31 AM
18/11/2023	7	11:39 AM		18/11/2023	6	12:12 PM
19/11/2023	8	12:18 PM		19/11/2023	7	12:44 PM
20/11/2023	9	12:52 PM		20/11/2023	8	1:10 PM
21/11/2023	10	1:23 PM		21/11/2023	9	1:32 PM
22/11/2023	11	1:52 PM		22/11/2023	10	1:52 PM
23/11/2023	12	2:22 PM		23/11/2023	11	2:12 PM
24/11/2023	13	2:53 PM		24/11/2023	12	2:34 PM
25/11/2023	14	3:27 PM		25/11/2023	13	2:58 PM
26/11/2023	15	4:05 PM		26/11/2023	14	3:27 PM
27/11/2023	16	4:49 PM		27/11/2023	15	4:03 PM
28/11/2023	17	5:39 PM		28/11/2023	16	4:48 PM
29/11/2023	18	6:35 PM		29/11/2023	17	5:42 PM
30/11/2023	19	7:33 PM		30/11/2023	18	6:43 PM

You can find the description of each lunar day in the chapter "A Guide to The Moon Cycle and Lunar Days"

This month, you are opening yet another door to the future. It is just what you dreamt of, but there are some clear shortcomings here. You will need November to fix them.

Work. For anything work-related, November is a great month. Your ties with colleagues in other cities and abroad are stable and moving along. You might engage in constructive negotiations, or perhaps go on a successful trip.

Your positive experiences with managers or auditing bodies help to smooth over some difficulties which will reveal themselves during the second 10 days of the month. That may involve claims from certain people, possibly financial or ideological in nature. However, there is nothing that can't be resolved, and this time, there is nothing stopping you from doing that this month.

Minor misunderstandings with a colleague from afar can certainly be fixed, your will, perseverance, and a bit of luck will be all you need, this time.

Money. Financially speaking, November is stable for you. Expect the largest sums to come in on November 1, 10-11, 18, 19, 27, and 28. Your expenses are still related to your children or loved ones.

Love and family. You might see squabbling in your personal life that occasionally breaks into a full-on argument. That is especially the case for unmarried couples, who will not be able to define how their relationship should look in the future. With characteristic caution, you are constantly going over everything in your mind. Did you do everything right? How will your relationship look? It doesn't really matter. Just let things be as they may, and don't pressure your partner. Just be glad he or she is there.

You may also have to put out some fires over the New Moon period from November 12-14.

Parents might have to solve problems involving their children. That may mean facing difficult tasks involving adult children's demands or spending more energy taking care of those who are still small.

After November 20, you might also face challenges related to your relatives. You are well-acquainted with these issues already, and there is nothing new here.

Health. Much of November will see you as healthy, energetic, and able to tackle anything that this month throws your way. You may feel a bit less vigorous during the last 10 days of the month, so try to stick to a schedule and remember to get enough sleep. Be careful when traveling and driving, too. This is especially pertinent during the last 10 days of the month.

December

New York Time			London Time		
Calendar Day	Lunar Day	Lunar Day Start Time	Calendar Day	Lunar Day	Lunar Day Start Time
01/12/2023	20	8:33 PM	01/12/2023	19	7:49 PM
02/12/2023	21	9:34 PM	02/12/2023	20	8:57 PM
03/12/2023	22	10:33 PM	03/12/2023	21	10:04 PM
04/12/2023	23	11:31 PM	04/12/2023	22	11:11 PM
06/12/2023	24	12:29 AM	06/12/2023	23	12:17 AM
07/12/2023	25	1:28 AM	07/12/2023	24	1:24 AM
08/12/2023	26	2:28 AM	08/12/2023	25	2:32 AM
09/12/2023	27	3:30 AM	09/12/2023	26	3:42 AM
10/12/2023	28	4:34 AM	10/12/2023	27	4:54 AM
11/12/2023	29	5:40 AM	11/12/2023	28	6:08 AM
12/12/2023	30	6:46 AM	12/12/2023	29	7:21 AM
12/12/2023	1	6:32 PM	12/12/2023	1	11:32 PM
13/12/2023	2	7:49 AM	13/12/2023	2	8:28 AM
14/12/2023	3	8:46 AM	14/12/2023	3	9:25 AM
15/12/2023	4	9:36 AM	15/12/2023	4	10:11 AM
16/12/2023	5	10:18 AM	16/12/2023	5	10:47 AM
17/12/2023	6	10:55 AM	17/12/2023	6	11:15 AM
18/12/2023	7	11:27 AM	18/12/2023	7	11:38 AM
19/12/2023	8	11:56 AM	19/12/2023	8	11:59 AM
20/12/2023	9	12:25 PM	20/12/2023	9	12:19 PM
21/12/2023	10	12:55 PM	21/12/2023	10	12:39 PM
22/12/2023	11	1:27 PM	22/12/2023	11	1:02 PM
23/12/2023	12	2:02 PM	23/12/2023	12	1:28 PM
24/12/2023	13	2:43 PM	24/12/2023	13	2:00 PM
25/12/2023	14	3:30 PM	25/12/2023	14	2:41 PM
26/12/2023	15	4:23 PM	26/12/2023	15	3:30 PM
27/12/2023	16	5:20 PM	27/12/2023	16	4:28 PM
28/12/2023	17	6:20 PM	28/12/2023	17	5:33 PM
29/12/2023	18	7:21 PM	29/12/2023	18	6:40 PM
30/12/2023	19	8:21 PM	30/12/2023	19	7:48 PM
31/12/2023	20	9:20 PM	31/12/2023	20	8:56 PM

You can find the description of each lunar day in the chapter "A Guide to The Moon Cycle and Lunar Days"

The last month of 2023 will not be an easy time for you. You will have to focus on your home, work, and various organizational tasks, as well. The stars advise you to keep a schedule and concentrate on what's most important.

Work. December is a time for you to get serious about administrative tasks, as well as certain relationships with people in your circle.

Your connection to colleagues in other cities or abroad is still something that requires a special approach, adaptability, and diplomacy on your part. Here, not everything will be going as planned, but you will be sure to see improvements compared to the past.

In order to resolve these problems, you may have to turn to an old friend, but you're the one who's going to have to do the heavy lifting. Fortunately, you're strong enough for it. This has happened before, so it won't be very difficult for you to handle.

Try to deal with any difficult tasks during the first half of December, because from the 13th to January 2, 2024, Mercury will be in retrograde and in your sign, too. You may tend to change your mind constantly and feel agitated and anxious.

Remember that it is not a good time to make any important decisions, sign any major documents, or start new projects! Remember that slow and steady is the way ahead right now and keep that in mind as you gradually resolve whatever comes your way. You will be able to avoid any problems and once again get back to the straight and narrow path toward success and prosperity in no time.

Money. December is fairly modest for your finances. You will not run into any unexpected gifts from fate, but whatever you earned with an honest day's work is not going anywhere, either. Your main expenses are related to your children and loved ones.

Love and family. This month, your personal life may keep you busier than work. You are doing everything you can to repair your relationship with your children, and you will make a lot of progress here. Most likely, things will quiet down, but you can expect some disagreements here and there.

In many families, you will continue to see difficulties involving relatives, but here, there is nothing new. There may be an old quarrel at play, or possibly a family member who is facing hard times.

Most couples are restoring balance to their relationships. There is no doubt about what your trump card is, here – you will make the first step to reconcile with your partner, and he or she will respond in kind.

Health. In December, you are not feeling as energetic as in the past, and that will be most noticeable during the New Moon from December 11-13. During this time, take care of yourself and avoid excessive eating or drinking. Stay away from any winter infections or colds, or a reappearance of old, chronic illnesses. Spend the holidays with your loved ones.

Capricorn Description

Sign. Feminine, earth, cardinal.

Ruler. Saturn

Exaltation. Mars, Pluto.

Temperament. Phlegmatic, with a strong tendency toward pessimism.

Positive traits. Goal-oriented, perseverance, has a strong endurance, restrained, has self-control, ambitious, proud, independent, industrious, efficient.

Negative traits. Selfish, capricious, ambitious, insidiousness, incredulous, cruel, greedy, is dissatisfied with herself, moody.

Weaknesses in the body. Knees, bones, skeleton, ligaments, tendons, digestive tract, liver, gallbladder, spleen, pancreas, skin, teeth.

Metal. Iron.

Minerals. For a talisman, black onyx. Generally – opal, blue sapphire, spinel, chalcedony, cat's eye.

Color. Black, blue-black, dark red.

Day. Saturday.

Capricorn energy

In ancient times, Saturn, the ruling planet of Capricorn, was associated with time. The ancient Aryans referred to it as Keyvan, the "lord of time". A calendar was built around Saturn's revolutions around the Sun (32 years), and it still survives today. The Saturnian calendar is not only for counting time, but also for spiritual protection from the heavens and gaining spiritual power. Saturn was revered as the god of the golden age. This means that every Capricorn is capable of rearranging the world, but it would be a mistake to assume that Capricorns are only focused on social revolutions. They start with their own world – their home, family, and themselves. Saturn's children tend to be withdrawn and isolated, as this is a planet of loners and ascetics. Capricorn's life is a journey of trials and self-improvement, but there is also a reward. Saturn allows individuals to slowly but surely achieve their goals through determination and patience. Capricorns always find their place in life and manage to settle down successfully. Capricorn is an Earth sign, and as a result is patient, practical, stable, and clear-headed. She will never miss out on any money-making opportunities, has her feet firmly on the ground, and a clear appreciation of reality.

Astrological portrait of Capricorn

Capricorn is fiercely independent. She is contemplative and analyzes and evaluates all of the events around her. She will not accept anything that she has not seen and heard with her own eyes and ears. She relies on her own strength and will not tolerate any meddling in her life. She is purposeful, and this may be Capricorn's most essential trait. She is very goal-oriented, and incredibly adaptable and tactical as she works to reach her target. She is never satisfied with what she has and continues to strive to reach the very top. She is brimming with ambition, and lives with a sense of higher purpose to achieve something special and change the world. Capricorn is steady as she moves ahead. She is very patient and not afraid of hard work. Sooner or later, almost all Capricorns end up in some sort of leadership position. They respect reliability, and to them, that means money. They are very good with money, never waste it, and always have savings. They aim for financial security and usually achieve it.

Many Capricorns are pessimistic or secretive, with high walls around them. Many are also ascetic and limit themselves in everything. But this is rooted in Capricorn's deep vulnerability. Despite her stiff upper lip and desire to be alone, Capricorn also needs affection. She suffers from her own isolation and is tormented by constant fears and pessimism. If that were not in her way, she might reach her goals twice as fast as she does.

Capricorn is high-minded and knows how to apply this to life. She is willing to sacrifice everything, including her own comforts, and to carefully plan her next step. She is able to worm her way out of anything, has a calm demeanor, and never loses control, no matter how tough things get. Many preachers, pastors, prophets, and missionaries are Capricorns. Her worst qualities are bitterness and irritability, as well as nagging doubt and indecision, along with a general distrust of others. From early childhood, Capricorn needs solid intellectual and spiritual development. Her life's path will be difficult, and for that, she needs personal strength as well as knowledge and money.

How to recognize Capricorn from appearances

Capricorns tend to be slender, but they are rarely very tall. They don't smile much and laugh even less. Their face seems rigid, even when they speak. They have pointed chins, and their eyes are either small and deep set or large. They usually have dark, sometimes curly hair. They are quiet and discreet, do not argue, and prefer to watch things play out from a distance as they draw their own conclusions. They don't talk about themselves much and are usually not the life of the party, though they are excellent at organizing and leading.

Charting Capricorn's Fate

It is unlikely that Capricorn will have a smooth journey through life. There are obstacles, ups and downs, worries, and fears. However, every cloud has a silver lining. Thanks to Capricorn's persistence, skill, and work ethic, she is able to achieve everything she plans, and even manage to enjoy her success, thanks to her longevity. As children and teens, they tend to be sickly, but this improves with age, as they become stronger and more resilient. Once they have overcome all of the hurdles in their way, Capricorns enjoy a period of prosperity that usually begins in middle age (40-50 years).

A Guide to The Moon Cycle and Lunar Days

Since Ancient times, people have noticed that the moon has a strong influence on nature. Our Earth and everything living on it is a single living being, which is why the phases of the moon have such an effect on our health and mental state, and therefore, our lives. Remember Shakespeare and his description of Othello's jealousy in his famous tragedy:

"It is the very error of the moon, She comes more nearer Earth than she was wont And makes men mad."

If our inner rhythm is in harmony with that of the cosmos, we are able to achieve much more. People were aware of this a thousand years ago. The lunar calendar is ancient. We can find it among the ancient Sumerians (4000-3000 BC), the inhabitants of Mesopotamia, Native Americans, Hindus, and ancient Slavs. There is evidence that the Siberian Yakuts had a lunar calendar, as did the Malaysians.

Primitive tribes saw the moon as a source of fertility. Long before Christianity, the waxing moon was seen as favorable for planting new crops and starting a new business, for success and making money, while the waning moon was a sign that business would end.

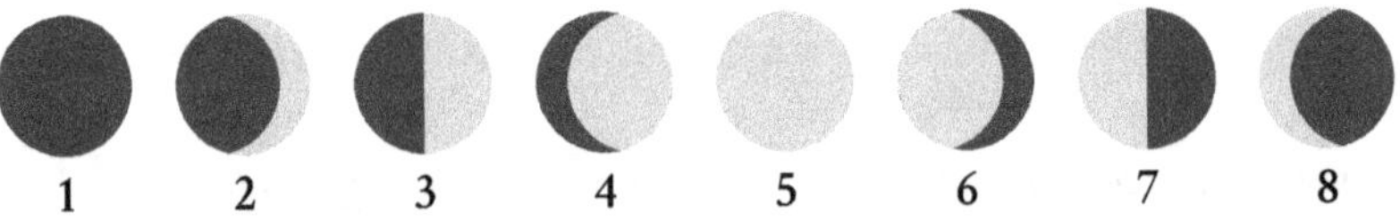

What are the phases of the moon?

- Phase 1 – new moon
- Phase 2 – waxing crescent moon
- Phase 3 – first quarter moon
- Phase 4 – waxing gibbous moon
- Phase 5 – full moon
- Phase 6 – waning gibbous moon
- Phase 7 – third quarter moon
- Phase 8 – waning crescent moon

To simplify things, we can divide the month into two phases:
Waxing crescent moon - before the full moon
Waning crescent moon - after the full moon

New Moon

We cannot see the new moon, as it is hidden. People might complain about feeling weak, mental imbalance, and fatigue. During this time, we want to avoid taking on too much or overdoing things. Generally, people are not very responsive and react poorly to requests, which is why it is best to look out for yourself, while not keeping your plate too full.

The new moon is a bad time for advertising – it will go unnoticed. It is not worth preparing any presentations, parties, or loud gatherings. People are feeling constrained, not very social, and sluggish.

This is also a less than ideal time for surgery, as your recovery will be slow, and the likelihood of medical error is high.

It is also difficult to get an accurate diagnosis during the new moon – diseases might seem to be hidden, and doctors might not see the real underlying cause of what ails you.

The new moon is also a bad time for dates, and sexual encounters may be dissatisfying and leave you feeling disappointed. Ancient astrologers did not advise planning a wedding night during the new moon.

Waxing Crescent Moon

It is easy to identify a waxing crescent moon. If you draw an imaginary line between the two "horns", you should see the letter P. The waxing moon is then divided into one and two quarters.

During the first quarter moon, we need to focus on planning – setting goals and thinking of how we will set about achieving them. However, it is still a good idea to hold back a bit and not overdo things. Energy levels are still low, though they are growing along with the moon. It is still a good idea to avoid any medical procedures during this time.

The second quarter is a time for bold, decisive action. Things will come easy, and there is a greater chance of a lucky break. This is a good time for weddings, especially if the moon will be in Libra, Cancer, or Taurus. Nevertheless, it is a good idea to put off any advertising activities and public speaking until closer to the full moon, if you can.

Full Moon

During the full moon, the Earth is located between the sun and the moon. During this time, the moon is round and fully illuminated. This takes place during days 14-16 of the lunar cycle.

During the full moon, many people feel more vigorous than usual. They are emotional, sociable, and actively seeking more contact, so this may be a good time for any celebrations.

However, be careful not to drink too much – you can relax to the point that you lose control, and the consequences of that can be very unpleasant. If you are able to stick to moderation, there is no better time for a party!

The full moon is also the best time for advertising, as not only will your campaign be widely seen, people will be apt to remember it.

The full moon is also a favorable time for dates, and during this time, people are at their most open, romantic, and willing to tell each other something important that might take their relationship to the next level of trust and understanding.

Moreover, during the full moon, people feel a surge of energy, which may lead to hyperactivity, restlessness, and insomnia.

It will be harder to keep your emotions in check. You might face conflicts with friends, disasters, and accidents. During the full moon, any surgeries are **not a good idea**, as the risk of complications and bleeding is on the rise. Plastic surgery is also a bad idea, as swelling and bruises might be much worse than in another lunar phase. At the same time, the full moon is a good time to get an accurate diagnosis.

During this time, try to limit your calories and liquid intake (especially if you deal with bloating and excess weight), as your body is absorbing both calories and liquids faster during the full moon, and it can be very difficult to get rid of the weight later on.

Waning Crescent Moon

The full moon is over, and a new phase is beginning – the waning moon. This is a quieter time, when all of the jobs you started earlier are being partly or entirely completed (it all depends on the speed and scale).

Surgery will turn out much better if it is performed during the waning moon. Your recovery will be faster, and the likelihood of complications is much lower. If you have any plans to lose weight, the waning moon is the best time to do that. This is also a good time for quitting bad habits, such as smoking or cursing.

The waning moon can also be divided into the third and fourth quarters.

Third quarter - this is a favorable period, and you are able to resolve a lot of problems without conflict. People are calming down and ready to listen and take in information, while still being active. However, this is not the best time to begin any major projects, especially if you are unsure if you will be able to complete them by the start of the new lunar month.

The third quarter is a good time to get married, especially if the moon is in Cancer, Taurus, or Libra.

Fourth quarter – This is the most passive period of the lunar cycle. You are not as strong as usual. Your energy is lagging. You will be tired until reaching a new beginning. The best thing you can do as the lunar cycle comes to an end is to get things in order, and avoid anything that might get in your way at work or in personal relationships. Examine your successes and failures.

Now, let's discuss the lunar days in greater detail. For centuries, people around the world have described the influence of lunar days, and modern astrologers only add to this work, as they compare old texts to modern life.

The 1ˢᵗ lunar day

The first lunar day is extremely important for the rest of the lunar month. This is a much-needed day to carefully plan your activities and lay the groundwork for the rest of the lunar month. Remember that the first lunar day is not a good day for major activities, but rather for sitting down and planning things.

Avoid conflicts on this day, unless you want them to overshadow the rest of the month. Try to see the positive side of things and imagine that the lunar month will bring you good things both at work and in love. The more vividly you can imagine this, the sooner your desires will come to fruition. Perhaps it would be a good idea to jot down plans that will bring you closer to achieving your dreams. This is the best time for both manifesting and making wishes!

This is also a favorable day when it comes to seeking a new job or starting an academic program.

It is fine to go out on a date on the first lunar day, but limit any sexual contact, as your energy levels are low, and you are likely to end up disappointed.

Getting married on the first lunar day is not recommended.

Avoid getting a haircut – there are many indications that cutting your hair on the first lunar day will have a negative effect on your health and life expectancy.

Under no circumstances should you undergo any major cosmetic procedures, including plastic surgery. Energy levels are low, your skin is dull and almost stagnant. The results will not live up to your expectations, and in the worst-case scenario, you will end up looking worse than before. It is common for cosmetic procedures performed on this day to be disappointing or even useless. Even the best surgeons are less capable.

Your good dreams on the first lunar day foretell happiness and joy. Bad ones usually do not come true.

The 2ⁿᵈ lunar day

This is considered a lucky day, and is symbolized by a cornucopia. It is not an exaggeration to say that the second lunar day is a favorable time for both work and love. It is a time for action, and a great period to work on yourself, look for a new job, start something new, or complete any financial transaction, whether a sale or purchase. This is also a great time for creative and scientific insights, and a good time for any meeting – whether political or romantic.

Any romantic dates or sexual encounters during the second lunar day are unlikely to disappoint. This is also a good day for weddings or taking a trip with someone special.

During the second lunar day, the moon is beginning its waxing phase, which is a good time for anything you might to do nourish and restore your skin. This is a great time for any cosmetic procedures aimed at preservation, though it is best to put off any plastic surgery until the waning moon. If that is not possible, then the second lunar day is acceptable, if not ideal, and you will not run into any complications.

Folklore tells us that this is not a good day for a haircut, as that may lead to arguments with a loved one.

This is the best time for exercise – your body is in good shape, and you are able to handle new exercise regimens. If the moon happens to be in Scorpio, though, be careful.

This is a good day for anything positive, but avoid any conflicts, discussions about the status of your relationship, or litigation.

Dreams of the second lunar day are usually not prophetic.

The 3rd lunar day

On this day, we are usually able to make out a thin sliver of the lunar crescent. It is a longstanding tradition to show money during the new month – it is believed that as the moon grows, so will your savings.

However, astrological systems around the world consider this an unlucky, unfavorable day. It is not a good idea to travel, begin any new business, or give into your bad mood.

You might run into many a lot of problems at work on this day, which will cause you a lot of anxiety. However, it is a good day to take a step back and identify and set about fixing any flaws and shortcomings. Remember that everything tends to look worse on this day than it actually is.

It is not the time to ask management for anything – you are likely to walk away disappointed, and end up unfairly reprimanded rather than receiving a promotion or raise. Instead, focus on areas of work that need to be smoothed over or studied further. It will be clear what problems you are facing, and you will easily be able to find a remedy.

Do not rush to criticize your loved ones – things may not be as they appear. "Measure twice and cut once" is your motto on this day.

This is not a good day to get married, as the couple is likely to have a turbulent, short-lived marriage.

You can schedule a cosmetic procedure for this day, but only if it is relatively minor. Plastic surgery should wait.

Do exercises as usual, without overdoing it or adding any new routines.

Dreams on this day do not mean anything.

The 4th lunar day

These are relatively neutral days, in that they are unlikely to bring anything bad, but they also will not bring you any windfalls. The fourth lunar day is symbolized by a tree of paradise, the tree of knowledge, and the choice between good and evil. Things ultimately depend on us and our final decisions.

This is a great day for anything money-related – signing contracts, agreements, or even taking on credit. There are also a lot of contradictions on this day – on one hand, we are likely to receive money, which is a good thing, but on the other, we will have to give some of it away, which is never particularly fun or pleasant. There is good reason to consider all of your opportunities and possibilities before acting.

It is not a good day to get married, as the wedding will not be as fun as you had hoped. However, the fourth lunar day is, in fact, a good day for sex and conceiving a healthy child.

Be careful on this day if you happen to engage in any physical exercise, as it is not a good idea to overeat or abuse alcohol. Take care of yourself. Any illnesses which began on this day may be extremely dangerous, if they are not dealt with immediately.

Cosmetic procedures are not contraindicated, as long as they are to preserve your appearance. Plastic surgery can be performed if you truly feel it is necessary.

However, avoid getting a haircut, as it is unlikely to grow back healthily, and will become brittle and dull. However, if the moon is in Leo, you can disregard this advice.

Dreams may turn out to be real.

The 5th lunar day

Traditionally, the fifth lunar day is one of the worst of the lunar month. It is symbolized by a unicorn. Unicorns need to be tamed, but only a virgin is capable of doing so. Many people will feel drained on this day, or frustrated with themselves, those around them, and life in general.

Try to avoid arguments- any conflicts are likely to drag out for a long time, and then you may be overcome with guilt. This advice is relevant for both work and love.

Sexual encounters may be pleasant, but this is not a good day to plan a wedding, as it is likely to lead to a marriage full of unpleasant incidents.

Do not start any new businesses, or ask those around you for favors- you may be misunderstood and rejected.

It is fine to engage in physical exercise, but if you overdo it on this day, you may injure yourself.

Your energy levels are low. Cosmetic procedures may not be effective, and avoid any plastic surgeries.

It is good if you dream something connected with the road, trips or with movement in general. A bad dream might be a sign of a health problem which should be addressed.

The 6th lunar day

The symbol of the sixth lunar day is a cloud and a crane. This is a philosophical combination that suggests that it is not worth rushing things on these days. This is a very positive, lucky day for both work and love. Creative work will be especially successful, as will any attempts at opening a new business in your field.

The sixth lunar day is a good time for resolving any financial matters. There is one limitation, however – do not give anyone a loan, as they may not pay it back. But you can certainly sponsor and support those who are more vulnerable than you.

This day is a good time to go on a trip, whether close to home or far away.

This is also a good day for dates, weddings, and marriage proposals. Remember that energy is more romantic than sexual, so it is better to give the gift of roses and a bottle of champagne than hot, passionate sex.

It is a good idea to get some exercise, but do not overdo things, though you will probably not want to, either.

Cosmetic procedures will be successful, and you can even have plastic surgery performed, so long as the moon is not in Scorpio.

It is still a good idea to avoid getting your hair cut, as you might "cut off" something good in addition to your hair.

It is better to not discuss dreams as they are usually true. Your dreams of this day can remind you of something that needs to be completed as soon as possible.

The 7th lunar day

This is also a favorable lunar day, and it is symbolized by a fighting cock, which is an Avestan deity. Avoid any aggression on this day, and instead work on yourself, spend time at home or in nature. Avoid discussing the status of your relationship with anyone, arguing, or wishing bad things on anyone. Everything will come back to haunt you, remember, silence is golden.

Business negotiations and contracts will be successful. You can find support, sponsors, and people ready to help you in both words and deeds.

Lighten up with your colleagues and subordinates. Pay attention not only to their shortcomings, but also to their skills. This is a good day for reconciliation and creating both political and romantic unions.

The seventh lunar day is good for traveling, no matter how near or far from home.

It is also a favorable time for love and marriage.

Exercise moderately, and any plastic surgeries will go very smoothly, as long as the moon is not in Scorpio.

Dreams of this day may become a reality.

The 8th lunar day

The symbol for this day is a Phoenix, which symbolizes eternal rebirth and renewal, because this day is a great time for changes in all areas of your life. Your energy is likely to be high, and you want to do something new and unusual. This is a good time to look for a new job or begin studying something. Any out-of-the-box thinking is welcome, along with shaking things up a bit in order to improve your life.

However, avoid any financial transactions, as you may incur losses.

Avoid aggression. You can share your opinion by presenting well-founded arguments and facts, instead.

The phoenix rises from the ashes, so this is a good time to be careful with electrical appliances and fire in general. The risk of housefires is high.

Avoid any major financial transactions on the eighth day, as you may end up facing a series of complications. You can pay people their salaries, as this is unlikely to be a large sum.

This is a good day for weddings, but only if you and your future spouse are restless, creative souls and hope to achieve personal development through your marriage.

Any cosmetic procedures and plastic surgeries will go well today, as they are related to rebirth and renewal. Surgeons may find that they are true artists on this day!

You can try to change your hairstyle and get a fashionable haircut on this day.

You can trust your dreams seen on this day.

The 9th lunar day

The ninth lunar day is not particularly auspicious, and is even referred to as "Satan's" day. You may be overcome with doubt, suspicions, even depression and conflicts.

Your self-esteem will suffer, so don't overdo things physically, and avoid overeating or abusing alcohol.

This is a negative day for any business deals, travel, or financial transactions.

This is a particularly bad day for any events, so keep your head down at work and avoid any new initiatives.

It is better to avoid getting married on "Satan's" day, as the marriage will not last very long. Avoid sex, as well, but you can take care of your partner, listen them, and support them however they need.

Any cosmetic procedures will not have a lasting effect, and avoid any plastic surgery. A haircut will not turn out as you hoped.

Dreams of this day are usually prophetic.

The 10th lunar day

This is one of the luckiest days of the lunar month. It is symbolized by a spring, mushroom, or phallus. This is a time for starting a new business, learning new things, and creating.

The 10th lunar day is particularly lucky for business. Networking and financial transactions will be a success and bring hope. This is an ideal time for changing jobs, shifting your business tactics, and other renewals.

This is a perfect time for people in creative fields and those working in science, who may come up with incredible ideas that will bring many successful returns.

This is a very successful day for building a family and proposing marriage. This is a good time for celebrations and communication, so plan parties, meet with friends, and plan a romantic date.

One of the symbols for this day is a phallus, so sexual encounters are likely to be particularly satisfying.

The 10th lunar day is the best time to begin repairs, buying furniture, and items for home improvement.

You can exercise vigorously, and cosmetic procedures and plastic surgery will be very effective.

Dreams of this day will not come true.

The 11th lunar day

This is one of the best lunar days, and seen as the pinnacle of the lunar cycle. People are likely to be energetic, enthusiastic, and ready to move forward toward their goals.

The 11th lunar day is very successful for any financial transactions or business deals and meetings.

You might actively make yourself known, approach management to discuss a promotion, or look for a new job. This is an auspicious time for advertising campaigns, performances, and holding meetings.

Any trips planned will be a great success, whether near or far from home.

Romantic relationships are improving, sex is harmonious, and very desired.

Weddings held on this day will be fun, and the marriage will be a source of joy and happiness.

Exercise is a great idea, and you might even beat your own personal record.

This is an ideal time for any cosmetic procedures, but any more serious plastic surgeries might lead to a lot of bruising and swelling.

A haircut will turn out as you had hoped, and you can experiment a bit with your appearance.

You can ignore dreams of this day – usually they do not mean anything.

The 12th lunar day

This day is symbolized by the Grail and a heart. As we move closer to the full moon, our emotions are at their most open. During this time, if you ask someone for something, your request will be heeded. This is a day of faith, goodness, and divine revelations.

For business and financial transactions, this is not the most promising day. However, if you help others on this day, your good deeds are sure to come back to you.

This is a day for reconciliation, so do not try to explain your relationships, as no one is at fault, and it is better to focus on yourself, anyway.

Avoid weddings and sex on this day, but if you want to do what your partner asks, there is no better time.

Many may feel less than confident and cheerful during this day, so take it easy when working out. Avoid overeating, stay hydrated, and avoid alcohol.

The 12th lunar day is not the best for getting married or having sex, but the stars would welcome affection and a kind word.

Avoid getting a haircut, or any plastic surgeries. This is a neutral day for minor cosmetic procedures.

Nearly all dreams will come true.

The 13th lunar day

This day is symbolized by Samsara, the wheel of fate, which is very erratic and capable of moving in any direction. This is why the 13th lunar day is full of contradictions. In Indian traditions, this day is compared to a snake eating its own tail. This is a day for paying off old debts and returning to unfinished business.

Avoid beginning any new business on this day. It is preferable to finish old tasks and proofread your work. Information you receive on this day may not be reliable and must be verified.

It is worth resolving financial problems very carefully, and avoid arguments and conflict.

Do not change jobs on this day or go to a new place for the first time. Do not sit at home alone, though, go see old friends, parents, or older family members.

Minor cosmetic procedures are welcome on this day, but avoid any plastic surgery, as you may experience major swelling and bruising. Avoid any haircuts, too.

As a rule, all dreams will come true.

The 14th lunar day

It's a full moon! The 14th lunar day is one of the happiest, and it is symbolized by the trumpet. Pay attention – you may run into new, much-needed information. Networking will be successful, and you can confidently sign agreements, meet with people, and attend fun gatherings or other leisure activities. This is one of the best days for advertising, performances, and concerts, and those working in creative professions should keep this in mind, as should those who work in politics. Do not sit in place on this day – you need to get out and see others, make new connections, and try to be visible.

This is one of the best days for communication with and making requests from management, as your initiatives will be noticed and welcome. You might talk about a promotion, raise, or something similarly related to professional growth.

Couples will see their relationship is moving along well on this day, and it is also a good day for getting married.

Any sex on this day will be vigorous and memorable for a long time. The full moon is the best time for conceiving a child.

Any cosmetic procedures will be effective, but avoid any major changes to your appearance, as there is a high likelihood of bleeding and bruising. A haircut will turn out well.

Your dreams of this day will be more or less doubtful.

The 15th lunar day

It's a full moon! This day is symbolized by a serpent of fire. This is the energy peak of the entire lunar cycle, and a lot will depend on where you are focusing your energy.

You might face a lot of temptations on this day, for example, you might tell someone else's secret or your own to others, and come to regret it for a long time. The stars suggest exercising restraint in both your words and actions, as the 15th day of the lunar cycle is a day of deception and weaknesses.

This is a very active time, and many people might take unnecessary risks. This is not the best day for signing any agreements or contracts. For any performances, concerts, or advertising, however, this is one of the best days of the month.

You can get married on the 15th day, but only if you know each other well and have carefully considered your partnership, without any hasty decisions. This is also a favorable day for a second marriage.

Your romantic relationship is looking wonderful – you are on cloud 9, writing poetry, and deeply convinced of how right your partner is for you – and they feel the same way. It is important that this does not suddenly lead to an abrupt disappointment.

Avoid getting any haircuts on the 15th day of the month, as you may end up with a headache.

Conservative cosmetic procedures and creams will be very effective, but avoid any injections or plastic surgery today. Bleeding, swelling, and bruising are all but guaranteed.

Dreams on the 15th day nearly always come true.

The 16th lunar day

This day is symbolized by a dove. The full moon is over, and the moon is now in its waning phase. Usually, after the turbulent days of the full moon, people feel a bit under the weather. They are not cheerful, and want to avoid excess worry and give themselves a chance to breathe.

Don't ignore your body's wishes, take it easy with physical activities, and take some time for yourself. You might spend time in nature, in the forest, or at a country home.

The 16th day of the lunar month is a time for moderation in all areas – your behavior, eating, and even in your clothes. If you overate during the full moon period, now is the time to diet a bit or at least avoid fatty foods and meat.

This is not a promising day for resolving any financial matters. Keep your documents in order and get ready for any future meetings, instead. If you help a loved one, your good deed will come back 100 times over.

Avoid getting married today, as well as sex.

Cosmetic procedures are likely to be a success, especially if they are related to cleansing your skin, but it is best to avoid any plastic surgery or injections. Your body is not ready to accept them. A haircut will turn out as you hoped.

Any dreams are likely to come true, but that also depends on a correct interpretation.

The 17th lunar day

This day is represented by a vine and bell. It is a happy day and both successful and fun-filled. It is also a good time for negotiations, concluding small business deals, shaking up staffing, and creativity. However, you should keep in mind that the 17th day is only favorable for minor business, and you should avoid starting any major events.

Avoid any major financial transactions on this day. Do not give anyone money as a loan or borrow anything yourself, either.

Any travel, whether for business or pleasure, is likely to be a success.

The 17th day is a great time to get married, and an ideal day for dates. Any sexual encounters will bring you happiness and joy.

Avoid getting your hair cut on this day, but cosmetic procedures and plastic surgery will be a success. Women will look better than usual.

Your dreams are likely to come true in three days.

The 18th lunar day

This day is represented by a mirror. It is a difficult, and generally unpromising day, too. Just as the mirror reflects our imperfections back to us, we need to remember that moderation and modesty are key.

The 18th day is not a favorable time for any business meetings or financial transactions. You can, however work on jobs you already began. It is, however, a positive day for those who work in research or the creative fields.

Your motto of the day is to keep a cool head when it comes to your opportunities and the opportunities of those around you. This is relevant for both work and romantic relationships. It is not a good time to criticize others – any conflicts or arguments may lead to lasting consequences, which you do not need.

Avoid getting married on this day, as well as sexual encounters, which are likely to be disappointing. It is a good time to take a trip together, which will only be good for your relationship.

Avoid getting your hair cut, though this is a relatively neutral day for a haircut, which might turn out well, and though it will not exceed your expectations, it will also not leave you upset. Avoid any plastic surgeries.

Dreams on this day will come true.

The 19th lunar day

This is a very difficult day and it is represented by a spider. The energy is complicated, if not outright dangerous. Don't panic or get depressed, though – this is a test of your strength, and if you are able to hold onto all you have achieved. This is relevant for both work and love. On the 19th day, you should avoid taking any trips.

The energy of the 19th lunar day is very unfavorable for beginning any major projects, and business in general. Work on what you started earlier, get your affairs in order, think over your ideas and emotions, and check to make sure that everything you have done hitherto is living up to your expectations. Do not carry out any financial transactions or take out any loans – do not loan anyone else money, either. Do not ask your managers for anything as they are unlikely to listen to what you have to say, and make judgments instead.

This is a day when you might face outright deception, so do not take any risks and ignore rumors. Do not work on anything related to real estate or legal matters.

This is a very hard time for people with an unbalanced psyche, as they may experience sudden exacerbations or even suicidal ideations.

This is a very unlucky day to get married. Sexual encounters might be disappointing and significantly worsen your relationship.

Avoid any haircuts or cosmetic procedures or surgeries.

Your dreams of this day will come true.

The 20th lunar day

This is also a difficult day, though less so than the 19th. It is represented by an eagle. This is a good time to work on your own development and spiritual growth, by speaking to a psychologist or astrologer.

Avoid pride, anger, arrogance, and envy.

The 20th lunar day is a good time for people who are active and decisive. They will be able to easily overcome any obstacles, flying over them just like an eagle. If you have to overcome your own fears, you will be able to do so – don't limit yourself, and you will see that there is nothing to be afraid of. It is a good day for any financial transactions, signing contracts, and reaching agreements, as well as networking.

The 20th lunar day is a favorable time for those who work in the creative fields, as they will be able to dream up the idea that will open up a whole host of new possibilities. Avoid conflicts – they may ruin your relationship with a lot of people, and it will not be easy to come back from that.

This is a lucky day for getting married, but only if you have been with your partner for several years, now. Sexual encounters will not be particularly joyful, but they also will not cause you any problems.

Avoid getting your hair cut, but you can certainly get it styled. The 20th lunar day is a good day for those who are looking to lose weight. You will be able to do so quickly, and it will be easy for you to follow a diet.

Cosmetic procedures will be a success, as will any plastic surgeries.

Pay attention to dreams of this day as they are likely to come true.

The 21st lunar day

This is one of the most successful days of the lunar month, and it is symbolized by a herd of horses – imagine energy, strength, speed, and bravery. Everything you think up will happen quickly, and you will be able to easily overcome obstacles. A mare is not only brave but also an honest animal, so you will only experience this luck if you remember that honesty is always the best policy.

This is also a favorable day for business. Reaching new agreements and signing contracts, or dealing with foreign partners – it is all likely to be a success. Any financial issues will be resolved successfully.

Those in the creative world will be able to show off their talent and be recognized for their work. Anyone involved in the performing arts can expect success, luck, and recognition. A galloping herd of horses moves quickly, so you might transition to a new job, move to a new apartment, or go on a business trip or travel with your better half.

The 21st lunar day is one of the best to get married or have a sexual encounter.

This is a great time for athletes, hunters, and anyone who likes adventurous activities.

But for criminals and thieves, this is not a lucky or happy day – they will quickly be brought to justice.

Any haircuts or cosmetic procedures are likely to be a huge success and bring both beauty and happiness. You will recover quickly after any surgeries, perhaps without any swelling or bruising at all.

Dreams tend to not be reliable.

The 22nd lunar day

This day will be strange and contradictory. It is symbolized by the elephant Ganesha. According to Indian mythology, Ganesha is the patron saint of hidden knowledge. so this is a favorable day for anyone who is trying to learn more about the world and ready to find the truth, though this is often seen as a hopeless endeavor. This is a day for philosophers and wisemen and women. However, it is an inauspicious day for business, and unlikely to lead to resolving financial issues, signing contracts, agreements, or beginning new projects. You can expect trouble at work.

For creative people, and new employees, this is a successful day.

This is a good day for apologies and reconciliation.

Avoid getting married, though you can feel free to engage in sexual encounters.

For haircuts and cosmetic procedures, this is a fantastic day. Surgeries will also turn out, as long as the moon is not in Scorpio.

Dreams will come true.

The 23rd lunar day

This is a challenging day represented by a crocodile, which is a very aggressive animal. This is a day of strong energy, but it is also adventurous and tough. Your main task is to focus your energy in the right direction. There may be accidents, arguments, conflicts, fights, and violence, which is why it is important to strive for balance and calm.

Keep a close eye on your surroundings – there may be traitors or people who do not wish you well, so be careful.

However, this is still a favorable day for business – many problems will be resolved successfully. You are able to sign contracts and receive credit successfully, as long as you remain active and decisive in what you do.

This is not a day for changing jobs or working on real estate transactions or legal proceedings. This is not a favorable day for traveling, no matter how near or far you plan on going.

This is not a promising day to get married – things may end in conflict, if not an all-out brawl.

Sexual relations are not off the table, as long as the couple trusts one another.

Haircuts or cosmetic procedures will not turn out as you had hoped, so avoid them.

Dreams during this lunar day usually mean something opposite of what awaits you, so you can disregard them.

The 24th lunar day

This is a neutral, calm day that is symbolized by a bear. It is favorable for forgiveness and reconciliation.

This is also a good day for learning new things, reading, self-development, and taking time to relax in nature.

This is a great day for any type of financial activity, conferences, academic meetings, and faraway travel.

The 24th lunar day is a good time for love and getting married, as any marriage will be strong and lasting.

Cosmetic procedures and plastic surgery will be a success, and you can expect a speedy recovery.

Avoid getting a haircut on this day, however, as your hair will likely thin and grow back slowly.

Dreams of this lunar day are usually connected with your personal life.

The 25th lunar day

This is still another quiet day, symbolized by a turtle.

Just like a turtle, this is not a day to rush, and it is best to sit down and take stock of your life. This is a good time for resolving any personal problems, as the moon's energy makes it possible for you to calm down and find the right path.

This is also not a bad day for business. It is believed that any business you begin on this day is sure to be a success. This is especially the case for trade and any monetary activities.

The 25th lunar day is not a good day to get married, especially if the couple is very young.

This is a neutral day for sexual encounters, as the moon is waning, energy is low, so the decision is yours.

Avoid any cosmetic procedures, except those for cleansing your skin. This is not a favorable day for haircuts or plastic surgery – unless the moon is in Libra or Leo.

You can have a prophetic dream on this day.

The 26th lunar day

The 26th lunar day is full of contradictions and complicated. It is represented by a toad.

It is not time to start or take on something new, as nothing good will come of it. Avoid any major purchases, as you will later come to see that your money was wasted. The best thing you can do on this day is stay at home and watch a good movie or read a good book.

Avoid traveling on this day, as it may not turn out well.

The 26th lunar day is a negative day for any business negotiations and starting new businesses. Do not complete any business deals or financial transactions. Your colleagues may be arguing, and your managers may be dissatisfied. But if you have decided to leave your job, there is no better time to do so.

This is not a good day to get married, as both partners' expectations may fall flat, and they will soon be disappointed.

The waning moon carries a negative charge, so avoid any haircuts and surgeries, though you can get cosmetic procedures if they are relatively minor.

Your dreams will come true.

The 27th lunar day

The 27th lunar day is one of the best days of the month, and it is represented by a ship. You can boldly start any new business, which is sure to be promising. This is a great day for students, teachers, and learning new things. Any information that comes to you on this day may be extremely valuable and useful to you.

The 27th day is good for communication and travel, whether near or far from home, and no matter whether it is for work or pleasure.

This is also a good day for any professional activities or financial transactions. If there are people around you who need help, you must support them, as your good deeds will come back 100-fold.

Romantic dates will go well, though any weddings should be quiet and subdued. This is a particularly good day for older couples or second marriages.

The waning moon means that hair will grow back very slowly, but in general, you can expect a haircut to turn out well. This is a great day for plastic surgery or cosmetic procedures, as the results will be pleasing, and you will have a speedy recovery, without any bruising or swelling, most of the time.

However, beware if the moon is in Scorpio on this day – that is not a good omen for any plastic surgery.

Do not pay any attention to dreams on this day.

The 28th lunar day

This is another favorable day in the waning moon cycle, and it is represented by a lotus. This is a day of wisdom and spiritual awakening. If possible, spend part of the day in nature. It is important to take stock of the last month and decide what you need to do during its two remaining days.

This is a good time for any career development, changing jobs, conducting business, decision-making, and signing agreements, as well as going on a trip. You might conclude any business deal, hold negotiations, work with money and securities.

This is also a good day for any repairs or improvements around your home or apartment.

Anyweddingstodayshouldbesubduedandmodest,andrestrictedtofamily members only. A loud, raucous wedding might not turn out very well.

Your hair will grow slowly, but any haircuts will turn out very elegant and stylish. Cosmetic procedures and surgeries are not contraindicated. You will recover quickly with little bruising and swelling.

Do not take any dreams too seriously.

The 29th lunar day

This is one of the most difficult days of the lunar month, and it is considered a Satanic day, unlucky for everyone and everything. It is symbolized by an octopus.

This is a dark day, and many will feel melancholy, depression, and a desire to simply be left alone. This is a day full of conflict and injuries, so be careful everywhere and with everyone. If you can, avoid any travel, and be particularly careful when handling any sharp objects. Do not engage in any business negotiations, sign any contracts, or take part in any networking.

Astrologers believe that anything you start on this day will completely fall apart. For once and for all, get rid of things that are impeding you from living your life. This is a good time to avoid people who you do find unpleasant.

This is also a time for fasting and limitations for everyone. Do not hold any celebrations, weddings, or have sexual relations – these events may not turn out as you hoped, and instead bring you nothing but suffering and strife.

Avoid getting a haircut, as well, as it will not make you look more beautiful and your hair will come back lifeless and dull. Cosmetic procedures can go ahead, but avoid any surgeries.

Dreams are likely to be true.

The 30th lunar day

There is not always a 30th lunar day, as some lunar months have only 29 days. This day is represented by a swan. The 30th lunar day is usually very short, and sometimes, it lasts less than an hour. This is a time for forgiveness and calm.

You might take stock of the last month, while also avoiding anything you do not need around you. Pay back loans, make donations, reconcile with those who recently offended you, and stop speaking to people who cause you suffering.

This is a good time for tying up loose ends, and many astrologers believe that it is also a good day to start new business.

However, avoid celebrations or weddings on this day. Spouses will either not live long, or they will quickly grow apart.

Do not get a haircut on this day, though cosmetic procedures are possible, as long as you avoid any surgeries.

Dreams promise happiness and should come true.

A Guide to Zodiac Compatibility

Often, when we meet a person, we get a feeling that they are good and we take an instant liking to them. Another person, however, gives us immediate feelings of distrust, fear and hostility. Is there an astrological reason why people say that 'the first impression is the most accurate'? How can we detect those who will bring us nothing but trouble and unhappiness?

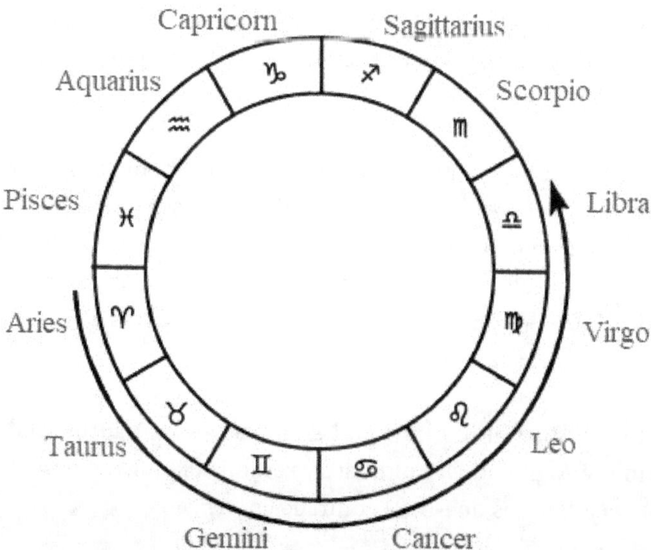

Without going too deeply into astrological subtleties unfamiliar to some readers, it is possible to determine the traits according to which friendship, love or business relationships will develop.

Let's begin with problematic relationships - our most difficult are with our **8th sign**. For example, for Aries the 8th sign is Scorpio, for Taurus it is Sagittarius and so on. Finding your 8th sign is easy; assume your own sign to be first (see above Figure) and then move eight signs counter clockwise around the Zodiac circle. This is also how the other signs (fourth, ninth and so on) that we mention are to be found.

Ancient astrologers variously referred to the 8th sign as the symbol of death, of destruction, of fated love or unfathomable attraction. In astrological terms, this pair is called 'master and slave' or 'boa constrictor and rabbit', with the role of 'master' or 'boa constrictor' being played by our 8th sign.

This relationship is especially difficult for politicians and business people.

We can take the example of a recent political confrontation in the USA. Hilary Clinton is a Scorpio while Donald Trump is a Gemini - her 8th sign. Even though many were certain that Clinton would be elected President, she lost.

To take another example, Hitler was a Taurus and his opponents – Stalin and Churchill - were both of his 8th sign, Sagittarius. The result of their confrontation is well known. Interestingly, the Russian Marshals who dealt crushing military blows to Hitler and so helped end the Third Reich - Konstantin Rokossovsky and Georgy Zhukov - were also Sagittarian, Hitler's 8th sign.

In another historical illustration, Lenin was also a Taurus. Stalin was of Lenin's 8th sign and was ultimately responsible for the downfall and possibly death of his one-time comrade-in-arms.

Business ties with those of our 8th sign are hazardous as they ultimately lead to stress and loss; both financial and moral. So, do not tangle with your 8th sign and never fight with it - your chances of winning are remote!

Such relationships are very interesting in terms of love and romance, however. We are magnetically attracted to our 8th sign and even though it may be very intense physically, it is very difficult for family life; 'Feeling bad when together, feeling worse when apart'.

As an example, let us take the famous lovers - George Sand who was Cancer and Alfred de Musset who was Sagittarius. Cancer is the 8th sign for Sagittarius, and the story of their crazy two-year love affair was the subject of much attention throughout France. Critics and writers were divided into 'Mussulist' and 'Sandist' camps; they debated fiercely about who was to blame for the sad ending to their love story - him or her. It's hard to imagine the energy needed to captivate the public for so long, but that energy was destructive for the couple. Passion raged in their hearts, but neither of them was able to comprehend their situation.

Georges Sand wrote to Musset, *"I don't love you anymore, and I will always adore you. I don't want you anymore, and I can't do without you. It seems that nothing but a heavenly lightning strike can heal me by destroying me. Good-bye! Stay or go, but don't say that I am not suffering. This is the only thing that can make me suffer even more, my love, my life, my blood! Go away, but kill me, leaving."* Musset replied only in brief, but its power surpassed Sand's tirade, *"When you embraced me, I felt something that is still bothering me, making it impossible for me to approach another woman."* These two people loved each other passionately and for two years lived together in a powder keg of passion, hatred and treachery.

When someone enters into a romantic liaison with their 8th sign, there will be no peace; indeed, these relationships are very attractive to those who enjoy the edgy, the borderline and, in the Dostoevsky style, the melodramatic. The first to lose interest in the relationship is, as a rule, the 8th sign.

If, by turn of fate, our child is born under our 8th sign, they will be very different from us and, in some ways, not live up to our expectations. It may be best to let them choose their own path.

In business and political relationships, the combination with our **12th sign** is also a complicated one.

We can take two political examples. Angela Merkel is a Cancer while Donald Trump is a Gemini - her 12th sign. This is why their relations are strained and complicated and we can even perhaps assume that the American president will achieve his political goals at her expense. Boris

Yeltsin (Aquarius) was the 12th sign to Mikhail Gorbachev (Pisces) and it was Yeltsin who managed to dethrone the champion of Perestroika.

Even ancient astrologers noticed that our relationships with our 12th signs can never develop evenly; it is one of the most curious and problematic combinations. They are our hidden enemies and they seem to be digging a hole for us; they ingratiate themselves with us, discover our innermost secrets. As a result, we become bewildered and make mistakes when we deal with them. Among the Roman emperors murdered by members of their entourage, there was an interesting pattern - all the murderers were the 12th sign of the murdered.

We can also see this pernicious effect in Russian history: the German princess Alexandra (Gemini) married the last Russian Tsar Nicholas II (Taurus) - he was her 12th sign and brought her a tragic death. The wicked genius Grigory Rasputin (Cancer) made friends with Tsarina Alexandra, who was his 12th sign, and was murdered as a result of their odd friendship. The weakness of Nicholas II was exposed, and his authority reduced after the death of the economic and social reformer Pyotr Stolypin, who was his 12th sign. Thus, we see a chain of people whose downfall was brought about by their 12th sign.

So, it makes sense to be cautious of your 12th sign, especially if you have business ties. Usually, these people know much more about us than we want them to and they will often reveal our secrets for personal gain if it suits them. However, the outset of these relationships is, as a rule, quite normal - sometimes the two people will be friends, but sooner or later one will betray the other one or divulge a secret; inadvertently or not.

In terms of romantic relationships, our 12th sign is gentle, they take care of us and are tender towards us. They know our weaknesses well but accept them with understanding. It is they who guide us, although sometimes almost imperceptibly. Sexual attraction is usually strong.

For example, Meghan Markle is a Leo, the 12th sign for Prince Harry, who is a Virgo. Despite Queen Elizabeth II being lukewarm about the match, Harry's love was so strong that they did marry.

If a child is our 12th sign, it later becomes clear that they know all our secrets, even those that they are not supposed to know. It is very difficult to control them as they do everything in their own way.

Relations with our **7th sign** are also interesting. They are like our opposite; they have something to learn from us while we, in turn, have something to learn from them. This combination, in business and personal relationships, can be very positive and stimulating provided that both partners are quite intelligent and have high moral standards but if not, constant misunderstandings and challenges follow. Marriage or co-operation with the 7th sign can only exist as the union of two fully-fledged individuals and in this case love, significant business achievements and social success are possible.

However, the combination can be not only interesting, but also quite complicated.

An example is Angelina Jolie, a Gemini, and Brad Pitt, a Sagittarius. This is a typical bond with a 7th sign - it's lively and interesting, but rather stressful. Although such a couple may quarrel and even part from time to time, never do they lose interest in each other.

This may be why this combination is more stable in middle-age when there is an understanding of the true nature of marriage and partnership. In global, political terms, this suggests a state of eternal tension - a cold war - for example between Yeltsin (Aquarius) and Bill Clinton (Leo).

Relations with our **9th sign** are very good; they are our teacher and advisor - one who reveals things we are unaware of and our relationships with them very often involve travel or re-location. The combination can lead to spiritual growth and can be beneficial in terms of business.

Although, for example, Trump and Putin are political opponents, they can come to an understanding and even feel a certain sympathy for each other because Putin is a Libra while Trump is a Gemini, his 9th sign.

This union is also quite harmonious for conjugal and romantic relationships.

We treat our **3rd sign** somewhat condescendingly. They are like our younger siblings; we teach them and expect them to listen attentively. Our younger brothers and sisters are more often than not born under this sign. In terms of personal and sexual relationships, the union is not very inspiring and can end quickly, although this is not always the case. In terms of business, it is fairly average as it often connects partners from different cities or countries.

We treat our **5th sign** as a child and we must take care of them accordingly. The combination is not very good for business, however, since our 5th sign triumphs over us in terms of connections and finances, and thereby gives us very little in return save for love or sympathy. However, they are very good for family and romantic relationships, especially if the 5th sign is female. If a child is born as a 5th sign to their parents, their relationship will be a mutually smooth, loving and understanding one that lasts a lifetime.

Our **10th sign** is a born leader. Depending on the spiritual level of those involved, both pleasant and tense relations are possible; the relationship is often mutually beneficial in the good times but mutually disruptive in the bad times. In family relations, our 10th sign always tries to lead and will do so according to their intelligence and upbringing.

Our **4th sign** protects our home and can act as a sponsor to strengthen our financial or moral positions. Their advice should be heeded in all cases as it can be very effective, albeit very unobtrusive. If a woman takes this role, the relationship can be long and romantic, since all the spouse's wishes are usually met one way or another. Sometimes, such couples achieve great social success; for instance, Hilary Clinton, a Scorpio is the 4th sign to Bill Clinton, a Leo. On the other hand, if the husband is the 4th sign for his wife, he tends to be henpecked. There is often a strong sexual attraction. Our 4th sign can improve our living conditions and care for us in a parental way. If a child is our 4th sign, they are close to us and support us affectionately.

Relations with our **11th sign** are often either friendly or patronizing; we treat them reverently, while they treat us with friendly condescension. Sometimes, these relationships develop in an 'older brother' or 'high-ranking friend' sense; indeed, older brothers and sisters are often our 11th sign. In terms of personal and sexual relationships, our 11th sign is always inclined to enslave us. This tendency is most clearly manifested in such alliances as Capricorn and Pisces or Leo and Libra. A child who is the 11th sign to their parents will achieve greater success than their parents, but this will only make the parents proud.

Our **2nd sign** should bring us financial or other benefits; we receive a lot from them in both our business and our family life. In married couples, the 2nd sign usually looks after the financial situation for the benefit of the family. Sexual attraction is strong.

Our **6th sign** is our 'slave'; we always benefit from working with them and it's very difficult for them to escape our influence. In the event of hostility, especially if they have provoked the conflict, they receive a powerful retaliatory strike. In personal relations, we can almost destroy them by making them dance to our tune. For example, if a husband doesn't allow his wife to work or there are other adverse family circumstances, she gradually becomes lost as an individual despite being surrounded by care. This is the best-case scenario; worse outcomes are possible. Our 6th sign has a strong sexual attraction to us because we are the fatal 8th sign for them; we cool down quickly, however, and often make all kinds of demands. If the relationship with our 6th sign is a long one, there is a danger that routine, boredom and stagnation will ultimately destroy the relationship. A child born under our 6th sign needs particularly careful handling as they can feel fear or embarrassment when communicating with us. Their health often needs increased attention and we should also remember that they are very different from us emotionally.

Finally, we turn to relations with **our own sign**. Scorpio with Scorpio and Cancer with Cancer get along well, but in most other cases, however, our own sign is of little interest to us as it has a similar energy. Sometimes, this relationship can develop as a rivalry, either in business or in love.

There is another interesting detail - we are often attracted to one particular sign. For example, a man's wife and mistress often have the same sign. If there is confrontation between the two, the stronger character displaces the weaker one. As an example, Prince Charles is a Scorpio, while both Princess Diana and Camilla Parker Bowles were born under the sign of Cancer. Camilla was the more assertive and became dominant.

Of course, in order to draw any definitive conclusions, we need an individually prepared horoscope, but the above always, one way or another, manifests itself.

Love Description of Zodiac Signs

We know that human sexual behavior has been studied at length. Entire libraries have been written about it, with the aim of helping us understand ourselves and our partners. But is that even possible? It may not be; no matter how smart we are, when it comes to love and sex, there is always an infinite amount to learn. But we have to strive for perfection, and astrology, with its millennia of research, twelve astrological types, and twelve zodiac signs, may hold the key. Below, you will find a brief and accurate description of each zodiac sign's characteristics in love, for both men and women.

Men

ARIES

Aries men are not particularly deep or wise, but they make up for it in sincerity and loyalty. They are active, even aggressive lovers, but a hopeless romantic may be lurking just below the surface. Aries are often monogamous and chivalrous men, for whom there is only one woman (of course, in her absence, they can sleep around with no remorse). If the object of your affection is an Aries, be sure to give him a lot of sex, and remember that for an Aries, when it comes to sex, anything goes. Aries cannot stand women who are negative or disheveled. They need someone energetic, lively, and to feel exciting feelings of romance.

The best partner for an Aries is Cancer, Sagittarius, or Leo. Aquarius can also be a good match, but the relationship will be rather friendly in nature. Partnering with a Scorpio or Taurus will be difficult, but they can be stimulating lovers for an Aries. Virgos are good business contacts, but a poor match as lovers or spouses.

TAURUS

A typical Taurean man is warm, friendly, gentle, and passionate, even if he doesn't always show it. He is utterly captivated by the beauty of the female body, and can find inspiration in any woman. A Taurus has such excess physical and sexual prowess, that to him, sex is a way to relax and calm down. He is the most passionate and emotional lover of the Zodiac, but he expects his partner to take the initiative, and if she doesn't, he will easily find someone else. Taureans rarely divorce, and are true to the end – if not sexually, at least spiritually. They are secretive, keep their cards close, and may have secret lovers. If a Taurus does not feel a deep emotional connection with someone, he won't be shy to ask her friends for their number. He prefers a voluptuous figure over an athletic or skinny woman.

The best partners for a Taurus are Cancer, Virgo, Pisces, or Scorpio. Sagittarius can show a Taurus real delights in both body and spirit, but they are unlikely to make it down the aisle. They can have an interesting relationship with an Aquarius – these signs are very different, but sometimes can spend their lives together. They might initially feel attracted to an Aries, before rejecting her.

GEMINI

The typical Gemini man is easygoing and polite. He is calm, collected, and analytical. For a Gemini, passion is closely linked to intellect, to the point that they will try to find an explanation for their actions before carrying them out. But passion cannot be explained, which scares a Gemini, and they begin jumping from one extreme to the other. This is why you will find more bigamists among Geminis than any other sign of the Zodiac. Sometimes, Gemini men even have two families, or divorce and marry several times throughout the course of their lives. This may be because they simply can't let new and interesting experiences pass them by. A Gemini's wife or lover needs to be smart, quick, and always looking ahead. If she isn't, he will find a new object for his affection.

Aquarians, Libras, and Aries make good partners for a Gemini. A Sagittarius can be fascinating for him, but they will not marry before he reaches middle age, as both partners will be fickle while they are younger. A Gemini and Scorpio are likely to be a difficult match, and the Gemini will try to wriggle out of the Scorpio's tight embrace. A Taurus will be an exciting sex partner, but their partnership won't be for long, and the Taurus is often at fault.

CANCER

Cancers tend to be deep, emotional individuals, who are both sensitive and highly sexual. Their charm is almost mystical, and they know how to use it. Cancers may be the most promiscuous sign of the Zodiac, and open to absolutely anything in bed. Younger Cancers look for women who are more mature, as they are skilled lovers. As they age, they look for someone young enough to be their own daughter, and delight in taking on the role of a teacher. Cancers are devoted to building a family and an inviting home, but once they achieve that goal, they are likely to have a wandering eye. They will not seek moral justification, as they sincerely believe it is simply something everyone does. Their charm works in such a way that women are deeply convinced they are the most important love in a Cancer's life, and that circumstances are the only thing preventing them from being together. Remember that a Cancer man is a master manipulator, and will not be yours unless he is sure you have throngs of admirers. He loves feminine curves, and is turned on by exquisite fragrances. Cancers don't end things with old lovers, and often go back for a visit after a breakup. Another type of Cancer is rarer – a faithful friend, and up for anything in order to provide for his wife and children. He is patriotic and a responsible worker.

Scorpios, Pisces, and other Cancers are a good match. A Taurus can make for a lasting relationship, as both signs place great value on family and are able to get along with one another. A Sagittarius will result in fights and blowouts from the very beginning, followed by conflicts and breakups. The Sagittarius will suffer the most. Marriage to an Aries isn't off the table, but it won't last very long.

LEO

A typical Leo is handsome, proud, and vain, with a need to be the center of attention at all times. They often pretend to be virtuous, until they are able to actually master it. They crave flattery, and prefer women who comply and cater to them. Leos demand unconditional obedience, and constant approval. When a Leo is in love, he is fairly sexual, and capable of being devoted and faithful. Cheap love affairs are not his thing, and Leos are highly aware of how expensive it is to divorce. They make excellent fathers. A Leo's partner needs to look polished and well-dressed, and he will not tolerate either frumpiness or nerds.

Aries, Sagittarius, and Gemini make for good matches. Leos are often very beguiling to Libras; this is the most infamous astrological "master-slave" pairing. Leos are also inexplicably drawn to Pisces – this is the only sign capable of taming them. A Leo and Virgo will face a host of problems sooner or later, and they might be material in nature. The Virgo will attempt to conquer him, and if she does, a breakup is inevitable.

VIRGO

Virgo is a highly intellectual sign, who likes to take a step back and spend his time studying the big picture. But love inherently does not lend itself to analysis, and this can leave Virgos feeling perplexed. While Virgo is taking his time, studying the object of his affection, someone else will swoop in and take her away, leaving him bitterly disappointed. Perhaps for that reason, Virgos tend to marry late, but once they are married, they remain true, and hardly ever initiate divorce. In bed, they are modest and reserved, as they see sex as some sort of quirk of nature, designed solely for procreation. Most Virgos have a gifted sense of taste, hearing, and smell. They cannot tolerate pungent odors and can be squeamish; they believe their partners should always take pains to be very clean. Virgos usually hate over-the-top expressions of love, and are immune to sex as a mean s of control. Many Virgos are stingy and more appropriate as husbands than lovers. Male Virgos tend to be monogamous, though if they are unhappy or disappointed with their partner, they may begin to look for comfort elsewhere and often give in to drunkenness.

Taurus, Capricorn, and Scorpio make the best partners for a Virgo. They may feel inexplicable attraction for Aquarians. They will form friendships with Aries, but rarely will this couple make it down the aisle. With Leos, be careful – this sign is best as a lover, not a spouse.

LIBRA

Libra is a very complex, wishy-washy sign. They are constantly seeking perfection, which often leaves them in discord with the reality around them. Libra men are elegant and refined, and expect no less from their partner. Many Libras treat their partners like a beautiful work of art, and have trouble holding onto the object of their affection. They view love itself as a very abstract concept, and can get tired of the physical aspect of their relationship. They are much more drawn to intrigue and the chase- dreams, candlelit evenings, and other symbols of romance. A high percentage of Libra men are gay, and they view sex with other men as the more elite option. Even when Libras are unhappy in their marriages, they never divorce willingly. Their wives might leave them, however, or they might be taken away by a more decisive partner.

Aquarius and Gemini make the best matches for Libras. Libra can also easily control an independent Sagittarius, and can easily fall under the influence of a powerful and determined Leo, before putting all his strength and effort into breaking free. Relationships with Scorpios are difficult; they may become lovers, but will rarely marry.

SCORPIO

Though it is common to perceive Scorpios as incredibly sexual, they are, in fact, very unassuming, and never brag about their exploits. They will, however, be faithful and devoted to the right woman. The Scorpio man is taciturn, and you can't expect any tender words from him, but he will defend those he loves to the very end. Despite his outward control, Scorpio is very emotional; he needs and craves love, and is willing to fight for it. Scorpios are incredible lovers, and rather than leaving them tired, sex leaves them feeling energized. They are always sexy, even if they aren't particularly handsome. They are unconcerned with the ceremony of wooing you, and more focused on the act of love itself.

Expressive Cancers and gentle, amenable Pisces make the best partners. A Scorpio might also fall under the spell of a Virgo, who is adept at taking the lead. Sparks might fly between two Scorpios, or with a Taurus, who is perfect for a Scorpio in bed. Relationships with Libras, Sagittarians, and Aries are difficult.

SAGITTARIUS

Sagittarian men are lucky, curious, and gregarious. Younger Sagittarians are romantic, passionate, and burning with desire to experience every type of love. Sagittarius is a very idealistic sign, and in that search for perfection, they tend to flit from one partner to another, eventually forgetting what they were even looking for in the first place. A negative Sagittarius might have two or three relationships going on at once, assigning each partner a different day of the week. On the other hand, a positive Sagittarius will channel his powerful sexual energy into creativity, and take his career to new heights. Generally speaking, after multiple relationships and divorces, the Sagittarian man will conclude that his ideal marriage is one where his partner is willing to look the other way.

Aries and Leo make the best matches for a Sagittarius. He might fall under the spell of a Cancer, but would not be happy being married to her. Gemini can be very intriguing, but will only make for a happy marriage after middle age, when both partners are older and wiser. Younger Sagittarians often marry Aquarian women, but things quickly fall apart. Scorpios can make for an interesting relationship, but if the Sagittarius fails to comply, divorce is inevitable.

CAPRICORN

Practical, reserved Capricorn is one of the least sexual signs of the Zodiac. He views sex as an idle way to pass the time, and something he can live without, until he wants to start a family. He tends to marry late, and almost never divorces. Young Capricorns are prone to suppressing their sexual desires, and only discover them later in life, when they have already achieved everything a real man needs – a career and money. We'll be frank – Capricorn is not the best lover, but he can compensate by being caring, attentive, and showering you with valuable gifts. Ever cautious, Capricorn loves to schedule his sexual relationships, and this is something partners will just have to accept. Women should understand that Capricorn needs some help relaxing – perhaps with alcohol. They prefer inconspicuous, unassuming women, and run away from a fashion plate.

The best partners for a Capricorn are Virgo, Taurus, or Scorpio. Cancers might catch his attention, and if they marry, it is likely to be for life. Capricorn is able to easily dominate Pisces, and Pisces-Capricorn is a well-known "slave and master" combination. Relationships with Leos tend to be erratic, and they are unlikely to wed. Aries might make for a cozy family at first, but things will cool off quickly, and often, the marriage only lasts as long as Capricorn is unwilling to make a change in his life.

AQUARIUS

Aquarian men are mercurial, and often come off as peculiar, unusual, or aloof, and detached. Aquarians are turned on by anything novel or strange, and they are constantly looking for new and interesting people. They are stimulated by having a variety of sexual partners, but they consider this to simply be normal life, rather than sexually immoral. Aquarians are unique – they are more abstract than realistic, and can be cold and incomprehensible, even in close relationships. Once an Aquarius gets married, he will try to remain within the realm of decency, but often fails. An Aquarian's partners need uncommon patience, as nothing they do can restrain him. Occasionally, one might encounter another kind of Aquarius – a responsible, hard worker, and exemplary family man.

The best matches for an Aquarius are female fellow Aquarians, Libras, and Sagittarians. When Aquarius seeks out yet another affair, he is not choosy, and will be happy with anyone.

PISCES

Pisces is the most eccentric sign of the Zodiac. This is reflected in his romantic tendencies and sex life. Pisces men become very dependent on those with whom they have a close relationship. Paradoxically, they are simultaneously crafty and childlike when it comes to playing games, and they are easily deceived. As a double bodied sign, Pisces rarely marry just once, as they are very sexual, easily fall in love, and are constantly seeking their ideal. Pisces are very warm people, who love to take care of others and are inclined toward "slave-master" relationships, in which they are the submissive partner. But after catering to so many lovers, Pisces will remain elusive. They are impossible to figure out ahead of time – today, they might be declaring their love for you, but tomorrow, they may disappear – possibly forever! To a Pisces, love is a fantasy, illusion, and dream, and they might spend their whole lives in pursuit of it. Pisces who are unhappy in love are vulnerable to alcoholism or drug addiction.

Cancer and Scorpio make the best partners for a Pisces. He is also easily dominated by Capricorn and Libra, but in turn will conquer even a queen-like Leo. Often, they are fascinated by Geminis – if they marry, it will last a long time, but likely not forever. Relationships with Aries and Sagittarians are erratic, though initially, things can seem almost perfect.

Women

ARIES

Aries women are leaders. They are decisive, bold, and very protective. An Aries can take initiative and is not afraid to make the first move. Her ideal man is strong, and someone she can admire. But remember, at the slightest whiff of weakness, she will knock him off his pedestal. She does not like dull, whiny men, and thinks that there is always a way out of any situation. If she loves someone, she will be faithful. Aries women are too honest to try leading a double life. They are possessive, jealous, and not only will they not forgive those who are unfaithful, their revenge may be brutal; they know no limits. If you can handle an Aries, don't try to put her in a cage; it is best to give her a long leash. Periodically give her some space – then she will seek you out herself. She is sexual, and believe that anything goes in bed.

Her best partners are a Sagittarius or Leo. A Libra can make a good match after middle age, once both partners have grown wiser and settled down a bit. Gemini and Aquarius are only good partners during the initial phase, when everything is still new, but soon enough, they will lose interest in each other. Scorpios are good matches in bed, but only suitable as lovers.

TAURUS

Taurean women possess qualities that men often dream about, but rarely find in the flesh – they are soft, charming, practical, and reliable – they are very caring and will support their partner in every way. A Taurus is highly sexual, affectionate, and can show a man how to take pleasure to new heights. She is also strong and intense. If she is in love, she will be faithful. But when love fades away, she might find someone else on the side, though she will still fight to save her marriage, particularly if her husband earns good money. A Taurus will not tolerate a man who is disheveled or disorganized, and anyone dating her needs to always be on his toes. She will expect gifts, and likes being taken to expensive restaurants, concerts, and other events. If you argue, try to make the first peace offering, because a Taurus finds it very hard to do so – she might withdraw and ruminate for a long time. Never air your dirty laundry; solve all your problems one-on-one.

Scorpio, Virgo, Capricorn, and Cancer make the best matches. A relationship with an Aries or Sagittarius would be difficult. There is little attraction between a Taurus and a Leo, and initially Libras can make for a good partner in bed, but things will quickly cool off and fall apart. A Taurus and Aquarius make an interesting match – despite the difference in signs, their relationships are often lasting, and almost lifelong.

GEMINI

Gemini women are social butterflies, outgoing, and they easily make friends, and then break off the friendship, if people do not hold their interest. A Gemini falls in love hard, is very creative, and often fantasizes about the object of her affection. She is uninterested in sex without any attachment, loves to flirt, and, for the most part, is not particularly affectionate. She dreams of a partner who is her friend, lover, and a romantic, all at once. A Gemini has no use for a man who brings nothing to the table intellectually. That is a tall order, so Geminis often divorce and marry several times. Others simply marry later in life. Once you have begun a life together, do not try to keep her inside – she needs to travel, explore, socialize, attend events and go to the theater. She cannot tolerate possessive men, so avoid giving her the third degree, and remember that despite her flirtatious and social nature, she is, in fact, faithful – as long as you keep her interested and she is in love. Astrologists believe that Geminis do not know what they need until age 29 or 30, so it is best to hold off on marriage until then.

Leo and Libra make the best matches. A relationship with a Cancer is likely, though complex, and depends solely on the Cancer's affection. A Gemini and Sagittarius can have an interesting, dynamic relationship, but these are two restless signs, which might only manage to get together after ages 40-45, once they have had enough thrills out of life and learned to be patient. Relationships with a Capricorn are very difficult, and almost never happen. The honeymoon stage can be wonderful with a Scorpio, but each partner will eventually go their own way, before ending things. A Gemini and Pisces union can also be very interesting – they are drawn to each other, and can have a wonderful relationship, but after a while, the cracks start to show and things will fall apart. An Aquarius is also not a bad match, but they will have little sexual chemistry.

CANCER

Cancers can be divided into two opposing groups. The first includes a sweet and gentle creature who is willing to dedicate her life to her husband and children. She is endlessly devoted to her husband, especially if he makes a decent living and remains faithful. She views all men as potential husbands, which means it is dangerous to strike up a relationship with her if your intentions are not serious; she can be anxious and clingy, sensitive and prone to crying. It is better to break things to her gently, rather than directly spitting out the cold, hard truth. She wants a man who can be a provider, though she often earns well herself. She puts money away for a rainy day, and knows how to be thrifty, for the sake of others around her, rather than only for herself. She is an excellent cook and capable of building an inviting home for her loved ones. She is enthusiastic in bed, a wonderful wife, and a caring mother.

The second type of Cancer is neurotic, and capable of creating a living hell for those around her. She believes that the world is her enemy, and manages to constantly find new intrigue and machinations.

Another Cancer, Virgo, Taurus, Scorpio, and Pisces make the best matches. A Cancer can often fall in love with a Gemini, but eventually, things will grow complicated, as she will be exhausted by a Gemini's constant mood swings and cheating. A Cancer and Sagittarius will initially have passionate sex, but things will quickly cool off. A relationship with a Capricorn is a real possibility, but only later in life, as while they are young, they are likely to fight and argue constantly. Cancer can also have a relationship with an Aries, but this will not be easy.

LEO

Leos are usually beautiful or charming, and outwardly sexual. And yet, appearances can be deceiving – they are not actually that interested in sex. Leo women want to be the center of attention and men running after them boosts their self-esteem, but they are more interested in their career, creating something new, and success than sex. They often have high-powered careers and are proud of their own achievements. Their partners need to be strong; if a Leo feels a man is weak, she can carry him herself for a while- before leaving him. It is difficult for her to find a partner for life, as chivalrous knights are a dying breed, and she is not willing to compromise. If you are interested in a Leo, take the initiative, admire her, and remember that even a queen is still a woman. Timid men or tightwads need not apply. Leos like to help others, but they don't need a walking disaster in their life. If they are married and in love, they are usually faithful, and petty gossip isn't their thing. Leo women make excellent mothers, and are ready to give their lives to their children. Their negative traits include vanity and a willingness to lie, in order to make themselves look better.

Sagittarius, Aries, and Libra make the best matches. Leos can also have an interesting relationship with a Virgo, though both partners will weaken each other. Life with a Taurus will lead to endless arguments – both signs are very stubborn, and unwilling to give in. Leos and Pisces are another difficult pair, as she will have to learn to be submissive if she wants to keep him around. A relationship with a Capricorn will work if there is a common denominator, but they will have little sexual chemistry. Life with a Scorpio will be turbulent to say the least, and they will usually break up later in life.

VIRGO

Virgo women are practical, clever, and often duplicitous. Marrying one isn't for everyone. She is a neat freak to the point of annoying those around her. She is also an excellent cook, and strives to ensure her children receive the very best by teaching them everything, and preparing them for a bright future. She is also thrifty – she won't throw money around, and, in fact, won't even give it to her husband. She has no time for rude, macho strongmen, and is suspicious of spendthrifts. She will not be offended if you take her to a cozy and modest café rather than an elegant restaurant. Virgos are masters of intrigue, and manage to outperform every other sign of the Zodiac in this regard. Virgos love to criticize everyone and everything; to listen to them, the entire world is simply a disaster and wrong, and only she is the exception to this rule. Virgos are not believed to be particularly sexual, but there are different variations when it comes to this. Rarely, one finds an open-minded Virgo willing to try anything, and who does it all on a grand scale – but she is rather the exception to this general rule.

The best matches for a Virgo are Cancer, Taurus, and Capricorn. She also can get along well with a Scorpio, but will find conflict with Sagittarius. A Pisces will strike her interest, but they will rarely make it down the aisle. She is often attracted to an Aquarius, but they would drive each other up the wall were they to actually marry. An Aries forces Virgo to see another side of life, but here, she will have to learn to conform and adapt.

LIBRA

Female Libras tend to be beautiful, glamorous, or very charming. They are practical, tactical, rational, though they are adept at hiding these qualities behind their romantic and elegant appearance. Libras are drawn to marriage, and are good at imagining the kind of partner they need. They seek out strong, well-off men and are often more interested in someone's social status and bank account than feelings. The object of their affection needs to be dashing, and have a good reputation in society. Libras love expensive things, jewelry, and finery. If they are feeling down, a beautiful gift will instantly cheer them up. They will not tolerate scandal or conflict, and will spend all their energy trying to keep the peace, or at least the appearance thereof. They do not like to air their dirty laundry, and will only divorce in extreme circumstances. They are always convinced they are right and react to any objections as though they have been insulted. Most Libras are not particularly sexual, except those with Venus or the Moon in Scorpio.

Leos, Geminis, and Aquarians make good matches. Libra women are highly attracted to Aries men - this is a real case of opposites attract. They can get along with a Sagittarius, though he will find that Libras are too proper and calm. Capricorn, Pisces, and Cancer are all difficult matches. Things will begin tumultuously with a Taurus, before each partner goes his or her own way.

SCORPIO

Scorpio women may appear outwardly restrained, but there is much more bubbling below the surface. They are ambitious with high self-esteem, but often wear a mask of unpretentiousness. They are the true power behind the scenes, the one who holds the family together, but never talk about it. Scorpios are strong-willed, resilient, and natural survivors. Often, Scorpios are brutally honest, and expect the same out of those around them. They do not like having to conform, and attempt to get others to adapt to them, as they honestly believe everyone will be better off that way. They are incredibly intuitive, and not easily deceived. They have an excellent memory, and can quickly figure out which of your buttons to push. They are passionate in bed, and their temperament will not diminish with age. When she is sexually frustrated, a Scorpio will throw all of her energy into her career or her loved ones. She is proud, categorical, and "if you don't do it right, don't do it at all" is her motto. Scorpio cannot be fooled, and she will not forgive any cheating. Will she cheat herself? Yes! But it will not break up her family, and she will attempt to keep it a secret. Scorpios are usually attractive to men, even if they are not particularly beautiful. They keep a low profile, though they always figure out their partner, and give them some invisible sign. There is also another, selfish type of Scorpio, who will use others for as long as they need them, before unceremoniously casting them aside.

Taurus is a good match; they will have excellent sexual chemistry and understand each other. Scorpio and Gemini are drawn to each other, but are unlikely to stay together long enough to actually get married. Cancer can be a good partner as well, but Cancers are possessive, while Scorpios do not like others meddling in their affairs, though they can later resolve their arguments in bed. Scorpio and Leo are often found together, but their relationship can also be very complicated. Leos are animated and chipper, while Scorpios, who are much deeper and more stubborn, see Leos as not particularly serious or reliable. One good example of this is Bill (a Leo) and Hillary (a Scorpio) Clinton. Virgo can also make a good partner, but when Scorpio seemingly lacks emotions, he will look for them elsewhere. Relationships with Lira are strange and very rare. Scorpio sees Libra as too insecure, and Libra does not appreciate Scorpio's rigidity. Two Scorpios together make an excellent marriage! Sagittarius and Scorpio are unlikely to get together, as she will think he is shallow and rude. If they do manage to get married, Scorpio's drive and persistence is the only thing that will make the marriage last. Capricorn is also not a bad match, and while Scorpio finds Aquarius attractive, they will rarely get married, as they are simply speaking different languages! Things are alright with a Pisces, as both signs are emotional, and Pisces can let Scorpio take the lead when necessary.

SAGITTARIUS

Sagittarius women are usually charming, bubbly, energetic, and have the gift of gab. They are kind, sincere, and love people. They are also straightforward, fair, and very ambitious, occasionally to the point of irritating those around them. But telling them something is easier than not telling them, and they often manage to win over their enemies. Sagittarius tends to have excellent intuition, and she loves to both learn and teach others. She is a natural leader, and loves taking charge at work and at home. Many Sagittarian women have itchy feet, and prefer all kinds of travel to sitting at home. They are not particularly good housewives – to be frank, cooking and cleaning is simply not for them. Their loved ones must learn to adapt to them, but Sagittarians themselves hate any pressure. They are not easy for men to handle, as Sagittarians want to be in charge. Sagittarius falls in love easily, is very sexual and temperamental, and may marry multiple times. Despite outward appearances, Sagittarius is a very lonely sign. Even after she is married with children, she may continue living as if she were alone; you might say she marches to the beat of her own drum. Younger

Sagittarians can be reckless, but as they mature, they can be drawn to religion, philosophy, and the occult.

Aries and Leo make the best matches, as Sagittarius is able to bend to Leo's ways, or at least pretend to. Sagittarians often end up with Aquarians, but their marriages do not tend to be for the long haul. They are attracted to Geminis, but are unlikely to marry one until middle age, when both signs have settled down. Sagittarius and Cancer have incredible sexual chemistry, but an actual relationship between them would be tumultuous and difficult. Capricorn can make a good partner- as long as they are able to respect each other's quirks. Sagittarius rarely ends up with a Virgo, and while she may often meet Pisces, things are unlikely to go very far.

CAPRICORN

Capricorn women are conscientious, reliable, organized, and hard-working. Many believe that life means nothing but work, and live accordingly. They are practical, and not particularly drawn to parties or loud groups of people. But if someone useful will be there, they are sure to make an appearance. Capricorn women are stingy, but not as much as their male counterparts. They are critical of others, but think highly of themselves. Generally, they take a difficult path in life, but thanks to their dedication, perseverance, and willingness to push their own limits, they are able to forge their own path, and by 45 or 50, they can provide themselves with anything they could want. Capricorn women have the peculiarity of looking older than their peers when they are young, and younger than everyone else once they have matured. They are not particularly sexual, and tend to be faithful partners. They rarely divorce, and even will fight until the end, even for a failed marriage. Many Capricorns have a pessimistic outlook of life, and have a tendency to be depressed. They are rarely at the center of any social circle, but are excellent organizers. They have a very rigid view of life and love, and are not interested in a fling, as marriage is the end goal. As a wife, Capricorn is simultaneously difficult and reliable. She is difficult because of her strict nature and difficulty adapting. But she will also take on all the household duties, and her husband can relax, knowing his children are in good hands.

Taurus, Pisces, and Scorpio make good matches. Aries is difficult, once things cool off after the initial honeymoon. When a Capricorn meets another Capricorn, they will be each other's first and last love. Sagittarius isn't a bad match, but they don't always pass the test of time. Aquarius and Capricorn are a difficult match, and rarely found together. Things are too dull with a Virgo, and while Leo can be exciting at first, things will fall apart when he begins showing off. Libra and Aquarius are both difficult partners for Capricorn, and she is rarely found with either of them.

AQUARIUS

A female Aquarius is very different from her male counterparts. She is calm and keeps a cool head, but she is also affectionate and open. She values loyalty above all else, and is unlikely to recover from any infidelity, though she will only divorce if this becomes a chronic trend, and she has truly been stabbed in the back. She is not interested in her partner's money, but rather, his professional success. She is unobtrusive and trusting, and will refrain from listening in on her partner's phone conversations or hacking into his email. With rare exceptions, Aquarian women make terrible housewives. But they are excellent partners in life – they are faithful, never boring, and will not reject a man, even in the most difficult circumstances. Most Aquarians are highly intuitive, and can easily tell the truth from a lie. They themselves only lie in extreme situations, which call for a "white lie" in order to avoid hurting someone's feelings.

Aquarius gets along well with Aries, Gemini, and Libra. She can also have a good relationship with a Sagittarius. Taurus often makes a successful match, though they are emotionally very different; the same goes for Virgo. Aquarius and Scorpio, Capricorn, or Cancer is a difficult match. Pisces can make a good partner as well, as both signs complement each other. Any relationship with a Leo will be tumultuous, but lasting, as Leo is selfish, and Aquarius will therefore have to be very forgiving.

PISCES

Pisces women are very adaptable, musically inclined, and erotic. They possess an innate earthly wisdom, and a good business sense. Pisces often reinvent themselves; they can be emotional, soft, and obstinate, as well as sentimental, at times. Their behavioral changes can be explained by frequent ups and downs. Pisces is charming, caring, and her outward malleability is very attractive to men. She is capable of loving selflessly, as long as the man has something to love. Even if he doesn't, she will try and take care of him until the very end. Pisces' greatest fear is poverty. They are intuitive, vulnerable, and always try to avoid conflict. They love to embellish the truth, and sometimes alcohol helps with this. Rarely, one finds extremely unbalanced, neurotic and dishonest Pisces, who are capable of turning their loved ones' lives into a living Hell!

Taurus, Capricorn, Cancer, and Scorpio make the best matches. She will be greatly attracted to a Virgo, but a lasting relationship is only likely if both partners are highly spiritual. Any union with a Libra is likely to be difficult and full of conflict. Pisces finds Gemini attractive, and they may have a very lively relationship – for a while. Occasionally, Pisces ends up with a Sagittarius, but she will have to fade into the background and entirely submit to him. If she ends up with an Aquarius, expect strong emotional outbursts, and a marriage that revolves around the need to raise their children.

Tatiana Borsch